AUTHOR MARKETING MAGIC

SELL LIKE A PRO AND BUILD LONG-TERM SUCCESS

M.L. RONN

Published by Author Level Up LLC.

Version 1.0

Cover Design by Pixelstudio.

Covert Art © drogatnev

Editing by BZ Hercules.

Special thank you to the following people on Patreon who supported this book: Olivia Williams, Plottr, BB Dee, Michael Guishard, Matty Dalrymple, Megan Mong, Sheila Klein, and Jon Howard.

Some links in this book contain affiliate links. If you purchase books and services through these links, I receive a small commission at no cost to you. You are under no obligation to use these links, but thank you if you do!

For more helpful writing tips and advice, subscribe to the Author Level Up YouTube channel: www.youtube.com/authorlevelup.

CONTENTS

WHAT YOU'LL LEARN FROM
THIS BOOK

Few things in the writing world are as opaque as marketing. Few things are also as simple as marketing. And yes, those statements contradict each other.

For some authors, marketing is the equivalent of a root canal; it induces sweat, tears, and frustration. Writing comes naturally, but marketing is challenging.

For another group of authors, marketing comes easily, sometimes more easily than the books themselves. These authors are effortless marketers; it seems that whatever they touch automatically mints money.

Most authors are somewhere in the middle. Marketing isn't easy, but it isn't hard. The keys are to devote the right time and energy toward it and to focus on the right activities for you.

Note the words "for you." Marketing is not one-size-fits-all. There is no book, course, webinar, guru, or secret white paper you can find that will make you an instant bestseller. If that were true, everyone would be making six and seven figures from their books.

When you consume any resource on marketing (including

this one), the best you can hope for is one or two actionable items that you can *try* to see if they make you money. The unfortunate reality about marketing in today's age is that much of what you do will fail. But when you do something that works, you should analyze it and determine if you should do more of it.

This book gathers many of the lessons I have learned in implementing just about every marketing tactic you can think of across my large book portfolio over the last decade. I'd like to share some frameworks that have led me to failure and success, sometimes at the same time.

While I hope this book makes you money, I hope it helps you avoid making mistakes and missing opportunities.

A LITTLE ABOUT ME

My name is M.L. Ronn (Michael La Ronn). I am the author of over 80 books of science fiction, fantasy, and self-help books for writers. I have been in the publishing scene since 2012. I have seen a lot of writers (and marketing tactics) come and go.

I also host "Author Level Up," a popular YouTube channel that, at the time of this writing, has over 40,000 subscribers. My videos have amassed over two million collective views on YouTube.

I am also the Outreach Manager at the Alliance of Independent Authors, a nonprofit organization for self-published writers whose goal is to help authors make better books and reach more readers. In my work with ALLi, I co-host a popular podcast called "The Self-Publishing Advice and Inspirations Podcast" (formerly known as the "AskAlli Member Q&A Podcast"), which is a monthly podcast where we answer the most burning member questions—many of which are about marketing.

I am also an in-demand speaker in the self-publishing community, having spoken on podcasts such as "The Creative

Penn" and "The Self-Publishing Formula." I have also spoken in person at the biggest author conferences in the world, including 20Books Vegas, Inkers Con, and Writer's Digest.

I built a writing career while raising a family, working full-time as an insurance executive, and attending law school classes in the evenings. Though I am not a full-time author yet, I am well on my way to getting there.

I am not an overnight bestseller, and I have had to work hard to reach my current level of success as an author. I hope that my background and approach will be useful to you. If you take away one or two things from this book, then I've done my job.

OVERVIEW OF THIS BOOK

You will find most major marketing methods covered here and a few things you may not have considered.

I will cover marketing basics, like the difference between marketing and promotion and what marketing is and is not. I will then cover the major components of every author's platform, including but not limited to websites, email lists, social media platforms, and more. I will also cover major promotion methods like paid advertising, email newsletter promotion services, and obtaining reviews.

At the end of this book, I summarize everything for you in a comprehensive checklist that you can follow for a stress-free book launch. I've also included a glossary for your convenience if you need more clarity on the various marketing terms I use in this book.

My greatest hope is that this book will help you become more confident in your marketing abilities. As Chris Fox says, we all start at zero. If you're not a marketing whiz, fear not, because we can all become one.

Onward, and let's have some marketing fun.

--M.L. Ronn
Des Moines, Iowa
October 11, 2022

IMPORTANT TERMS TO UNDERSTAND

Before we continue, I want to make sure that we are speaking the same language and that I am as precise as possible about what terms mean in this book.

This section (and the glossary at the end of this book) are powered by my book, *The Indie Writer's Encyclopedia: 300+ Terms You Need to Know as a Writer*. It contains all the definitions in this book as well as other writing, publishing, and business terms you need to know.

These are the most essential terms to understand, but there are more. If you come across a term that you don't understand or need more context, refer to the glossary at the back of this book for additional help.

ACTIVE INCOME

1.Income derived from activities that require ongoing effort

Active income activities include hand-selling books at conventions, author signings, and social media promotions, to name a few. Generally, to make money from these activities, you have to do them regularly and often.

CONVERSION

1. In marketing, the transformation of a prospective customer into a buying customer

COPYWRITING

1.In marketing and advertising, the act of writing advertisements that convinces a person to take a particular action

Copywriting is a completely different skill than writing a book.

Generally, authors write books to entertain or educate. Copywriters write to persuade people to buy, sign up for a mailing list, donate money, or do other necessary actions for a business to make money. Because it is a different skill, it requires a different mindset.

DIRECT SALES

1.The act of selling books directly on a website, or in person

Indirect sales are sales that happen at a book retailer, where the retailer takes a percentage of each sale, usually 30 percent to 40 percent for e-books and paperbacks. In a direct sales payment model, the author uses a payment transaction service that takes a very small percentage of each transaction, usually less than 10 percent. The royalties are higher, and the author can sell unique and inventive products that they would not be able to sell through a book retailer, such as merchandise.

DISTRIBUTOR

1.A company that distributes books from the publisher or author to book retailers

A distributor can distribute e-books, paperbacks, or audiobooks, though they usually specialize in one format. For print books, a "full-service" distributor offers a range of services, such as sales, inventory management assistance, operating warehouses, and goods delivery.

At the time of this writing, Draft2Digital, PublishDrive, and Streetlib are the most popular e-book distributors for indie writers, and Findaway Voices is the most popular distributor for audiobooks.

GOING WIDE

1.In self-publishing, the act of publishing a book on as many retailers as possible instead of being exclusive to Amazon

MARKETING

1.The act of selling a product or service

Marketing differs from promotion in that it is primarily about connecting with a target audience, crafting a message to speak to that audience, and creating packaging that will appeal to them. Promotion is the act of promoting the book to that audience, such as through advertising.

NICHE

1.A segment of the market whose audience has specialized interests and tastes

Niche is primarily a nonfiction term. You can't really achieve that level of specificity with fiction, but an example of a niche in fiction might be, for example, readers who like dark space opera along the lines of X author.

PARETO PRINCIPLE

1. Principle outlined by economist Vilfredo Pareto that 80 percent of effects come from 20 percent of the causes (such as 80 percent of sales come from 20 percent of an author's books)

The Pareto Principle is so fundamental because you can see it in every aspect of the writing life. Usually, 20 percent of an author's books will drive 80 percent of their sales. Usually, 20 percent of an author's readers will send 80 percent of the fan-mail.

However, the Pareto Principle is commonly mistaken as "you should spend 80 percent of your time doing X activity to get the best results," which is similar, but not the same.

PASSIVE INCOME

1.Income derived from activities that do not require ongoing effort

. . .

Passive income activities usually involve creating content once and letting it work for you, such as releasing a video that promotes an affiliate link. In fact, affiliate income is one of the most lucrative passive income strategies because you can create a lot of content around certain products and automate traffic through ads.

As a personal aside, I make affiliate sales from videos I made YEARS ago.

Other examples of passive income include low-maintenance online courses, and of course, book sales, though one could argue that book sales are passive-aggressive—if you don't do something to market your books, they will eventually fall off the radar, but even if you do nothing, you'll still probably sell some.

PROMOTION

1.The process of selling a book to a target audience

Promotion involves buying ads, talking to anyone who might be interested in a book, doing podcast interviews and guest blogs, and many more active tasks.

TARGET AUDIENCE

1.Group of people that are likely to be most interested in a business's product or service, based on their demographics, interests, internet activity, or history of buying similar products or services

MARKETING VERSUS PROMOTION

Marketing and promotion are often interchangeable, but they are not the same.

The Alliance of Independent Authors (ALLi) lays out a vision of "The Seven Stages of Publishing," which are the predictable steps every author takes when publishing a book.

The seven stages are as follows:

1. Writing
2. Editorial
3. Production
4. Distribution
5. Marketing
6. Promotion
7. Rights Licensing

ALLi treats marketing and promotion as two distinct phases of the process.

Marketing is the activities you do to let people know that your book is perfect for them. Promotion is the activities you do to let them know that the book exists.

Marketing is passive. It includes:

- positioning your book in the right subgenre
- identifying your target audience
- determining which tropes in your story will resonate most with readers in your marketing (and leaning into those tropes)
- designing your book cover
- setting the price for your book
- writing your book description
- determining the distribution channels for your book

If the task requires you to "push" the book to readers, then it is not marketing. It is promotion.

Promotion includes:

- running paid advertising
- giving interviews or speeches about your book
- guest blog posts
- doing a newsletter swap with another author
- attending local events to promote your book, such as an author signing event
- engaging with your community on social media (not just about your book)

The best way to think about the difference between marketing and promotion is to think about an iceberg. Eighty percent of an iceberg's mass is below the water. The remaining 20 percent is above the surface.

Marketing is everything you do below the surface that no one sees; promotion is everything you do that people see.

When we look at other authors and how successful they are at marketing, we often only see what they're doing to *promote* their work. We don't often see the decisions they made with their marketing, but we can if we dig deeper.

By understanding the difference between marketing and promotion, we can be more intentional about our daily activities.

My strategy has been to spend 80 percent of my time on marketing and 20 percent on promotion. If I don't get the marketing right, there is no amount of promotion I can do to help me. Building a solid foundation with marketing is critical.

Now that we understand the difference between marketing and promotion, remember—marketing should always come first!

WHAT MARKETING IS (AND IS NOT)

There are as many marketing styles as there are authors. For the sake of this book, I will assume that you struggle with marketing and want to do it better. You're probably not one of those marketing whizzes I talked about at the beginning of this book.

This chapter will cover some basics of what marketing is and is not.

MARKETING IS NOT TIME-CONSUMING (GENERALLY)

There is a misconception that you must spend a lot of time marketing.

How much time *should* you spend marketing?

Here is a rule of thumb. If you're spending all day every day marketing, that's probably not the answer. If you're spending zero time per day (or week) marketing, that's probably not the answer either. If you don't market frequently and spend a ton of time marketing in sporadic bursts, that's not productive.

The question remains: how much time *should* you spend marketing?

It depends on you and your needs. If you are comfortable

pounding the pavement and getting your book in front of people aggressively, then do that. However, if you are the type who prefers passive marketing, that's okay too.

But the key is to do *something*. Not necessarily every day, but every week. It adds up over time when you do it consistently, especially when you do the right things.

MARKETING IS SUPPOSED TO FEEL GOOD

If you dread a marketing task because you don't enjoy it, then don't do it. Only a few things are absolutely required in any author's marketing platform: designing professional covers, writing more books, building an email newsletter, and maintaining a good website. Everything else is optional.

Do you hate Facebook? A lot of people do.

Dread doing author swaps? Then don't do them.

Tired of attending author readings and local book fairs at libraries? Then stop.

The best marketing comes from tasks that you enjoy. If you enjoy a task, then you'll do it more and get good at it. If you're good at it, then you will be more effective. You get the idea.

If it doesn't feel good, then don't do it. I know that some marketing professionals will disagree with me on this point, but life is too short to spend your time doing things that you don't like, *especially* if you are a part-time author.

MARKETING IS NOT EXPENSIVE (MOST OF THE TIME)

Marketing doesn't have to break the bank. In fact, the best marketing is often free or low-cost.

Don't let anyone talk you into spending thousands of dollars on something that may not give you a guaranteed benefit.

There are a lot of people out there who want your money.

Keep your wallet locked unless it's a service that is worth it. "Worth it" means that other authors receive results, the company is ethical, you have realistic expectations about what you will achieve, and based on all the above, you have reasonable certainty that you will achieve those expectations.

If there is even a remote chance of buyer's remorse, then your gut is probably steering you in the right direction. Remember, you're only going to take away a few things from any marketing resource you purchase. Weigh that against the price tag.

Is one tip worth a $700 course? Probably not. Is learning *how* to do something that can make you money worth that same cost (like learning how to run your own Facebook ads, for example). Yes, that probably is. But usually, the marketing and promotion that gets you the best results will usually be on the cheaper side of things.

MARKETING IS NOT ROCKET SCIENCE

The best marketing is often easy to do.

I find that the simplest tasks generally have the biggest impact. Things like fixing the flow of your website, geo-locating links on Amazon, or updating the call to action in the back of your book can often yield better results than completely revamping your website or implementing a complicated autoresponder sequence, for example. If you're not selling many books, it may not be worth spending a bunch of time, money, and effort on a tactic that might not impact your sales.

If you have low-volume sales, then I would resist the urge to implement anything overly complicated until you can bear out the results with your sales data.

Simple is almost always better.

YOUR PLATFORM IS A SALESFORCE

Let me tell you a story.

My garage door stopped working, and I needed to buy a new one. I called four companies to get estimates.

The first company was the company that normally came out when my door malfunctioned. I liked them because they knew my house and had been there many times. When the salesperson visited, he wrote an estimate that was much higher than I expected, and he didn't do a good job of explaining what he was selling. For heaven's sake, he didn't even leave me any brochures! He told me they would install a "steel door."

At the time, I was having a busy day, and I was scattered. I had never purchased a garage door and didn't know what to ask. I forgot to ask about the panel design, windows, warranties, whether the door could be used with my existing opener, and other obvious questions the salesperson should have addressed.

The second company that came out sent a better salesman. He measured the door, asked me three questions, and handed me a brochure with the best options circled. He recommended the company's middle-tier garage door and explained why.

I liked the second salesman much better because he took the

time to explain what I'd be getting, but I didn't like the price. This was the largest company in the state and also a franchise, so I could tell they didn't really need my business. The salesman could tell I wasn't going to be a customer, so he ended the encounter quickly. The entire exchange took approximately five minutes.

The third company that came out sent a douchebag. He was pushy and only cared about selling me a garage door. I quickly sent him away.

The fourth company that came out sent an excellent salesman. This gentleman did everything the second guy did but asked me different questions. He explained some common problems I should have been thinking about. He also explained the nuts and bolts of garage doors. He was more experienced, and I can't quite explain why, but he put me at ease. I knew exactly what I was getting.

Which salesman do you think got my business?

If I had to classify the salesmen:

- Salesman #1 was the **Incompetent Salesperson**. He knew his stuff when it came to garage door installation and service, but he couldn't sell his way out of a paper bag. He also didn't understand his company's products.
- Salesman #2 was the **Typical Salesperson**. He asked key questions to determine if I was the right customer, and when he determined that I was not, he ended the visit.
- Salesman #3 was the **Douchebag Salesperson**. He didn't care whether I was a good fit—all he cared about was his sales quota.

- Salesman #4 was the **Excellent Salesperson**. Not only did he ask key questions to determine if I was the right customer, when he determined that I was, he took additional steps to close the deal. He was the guy I had been waiting for all along but didn't know it.

You might be thinking, "I want to be an excellent salesperson," but that's not where I'm going with this.

Yes, of course, you should be an excellent salesperson, but the reality in today's digital age is that you will do very little direct selling to readers, if any. Most of your "selling" happens automatically on your website or book's product page, often without you knowing about it.

So yes, while you do want to be an excellent salesperson, you also want your *platform* to be a superb sales*force*. That's much better.

Every element of your platform is a salesperson, and each one is working with the others to achieve the same goal: to get the right readers to buy your books.

Your website is a salesperson. Your call to action in the back of your book is a salesperson. Your email newsletter is a salesperson. You get the picture.

An excellent salesperson:

- knows their products
- exudes experience and wisdom
- anticipates what the customer needs and why they need it
- knows when to walk away from a customer
- knows when to keep engaging and how to close
- puts customers at ease

Does your website do all those things? Your email list? Your book description?

This is an entirely different way of thinking about sales, but it has worked wonders for me.

THE INCOMPETENT AUTHOR PLATFORM = MISSED OPPORTUNITIES

If your platform elements aren't set up correctly, they will be equivalents of the **Incompetent Salesperson**.

Your book might be *perfect* for the reader, but they won't know because:

- You bungled the opportunity by misunderstanding your book's genre.
- You failed to understand reader preferences and how they buy books.
- Your platform elements weren't organized logically, so readers left.
- You didn't sell enough.

In other words, you failed to help readers see why they should have bought your book.

Readers who aren't going to buy your book aren't going to buy your book no matter what you do. The real failure is the missed opportunity with the readers who would have been interested but didn't engage because your platform chased them away.

We all start with incompetent author platforms, but we can move to excellent ones by identifying the opportunities where we are missing out on sales.

The best way to identify these opportunities is to study the platforms of other best-selling indie authors in your genre.

Instead of seeing an idea and saying, "Oooh, I like that—I'll try it," instead think, "Is the tactic the author is using eliminating missed opportunities, and might *I* be missing those opportunities?"

Let me give you some examples.

Author A sells books directly to readers on their website. You do not. Therefore, you probably should because there will likely be readers willing to buy books directly from you.

Author B creates large print editions of their books. But, it turns out that readers in your genre don't buy large print books. Therefore, it probably doesn't make sense to do large print until reader tastes change. That isn't a missed opportunity.

So, look for missed opportunities. If you identify one, then you should seriously consider addressing it, but remember the rules I covered earlier about simplicity and cost. Some opportunities aren't worth chasing. As the cliché goes, the juice isn't worth the squeeze. But often, it is when you take a long-term view.

Suppose you think about your platform as a group of salespeople. In that case, you want them to be excellent salespeople who don't miss opportunities. It doesn't mean that they will make the sale every time, but they certainly won't *miss out* on any sales. That's the difference.

How many opportunities are you missing out on right now?

THE 8 ACTIONS THAT ALL READERS TAKE

When a reader discovers your book for the first time, they will take one of three actions:

1. They will buy the book.
2. They will not buy the book today, but will in the future.
3. They will not buy the book ever.

Your focus should be on those readers who defer buying the book. Those readers represent potential missed opportunities.

How do you do this? You must continue to get the book in front of them through advertising and other methods we will discuss in this book. But the average person usually sees a product multiple times before they buy it. That's critical.

When readers *buy* your book, they segment further into more categories:

1. They will love the book and become a true fan.
2. They will like the book, and want to engage with you further, but not on the level of a true fan.

3. They will like the book but not want to engage with you further.
4. They will not like the book.
5. They will hate the book so much that they leave a negative review, or worse–become a troll.

Look for missed opportunities among your readers.

I recommend always taking care of the readers who love your work. Don't waste your time on people who don't like your work.

The readers you should pay attention to the ones who like your work but who may not engage with you for some reason.

Why won't readers engage?

They could be busy. They might not have liked your book enough to continue engaging with you. Or—and this is what you want to prevent—they may not know that you have a mailing list, social media presence, or other books. That we have these things is obvious to *us*, but we have to do special work to ensure that readers are aware of our platform elements and how we want them to engage with us.

PUTTING YOURSELF IN READERS' SHOES

You also shouldn't discount your own experience as a customer. I recommend that you examine your own buying preferences. They may not align with best practices.

For example, email marketers swear by using "pop-ups," which are windows that pop up advertising your lead magnet, with enticing copy to get readers to subscribe to a mailing list. These windows usually appear as soon as you visit a website, sometimes on a time or scroll delay.

The mantra among marketers is that pop-ups are annoying, but they work. There have been plenty of studies by marketers that prove this point.

However, I find pop-ups annoying. I can't think of the last time I read one. When I did, the copy was usually so salesy and arm-twisty that I clicked away.

After examining my behavior, I decided not to use pop-ups on my website.

Another example: email marketing best practices indicate that you should email your mailing list subscribers regularly to prevent them from "going cold," which means they forget about you or become uninterested in your emails.

How frequently should you email your subscribers?

We are selling books, not services or high-end products. Because of this, I believe that emailing your newsletter subscribers every week is too much. I have been on author email lists where the author sent weekly emails, which I thought was annoying.

I have also been on mailing lists where authors only email every few years. That doesn't feel good either!

The answer is to find a middle ground. Email your subscribers when you have something new to share, but don't let it go too long between emails.

It's important to point out that your behavior as a customer may not match that of your readers. As you build a platform and talk to your readers, you will understand what they want. But if you don't know, it's not a bad idea to use your preferences as a map, as long as you don't miss opportunities.

Emailing your list frequently and making hard sells is very much an American internet marketer thing. As I've built a global audience, I have found that non-Americans despise hard pitches. I've had to soften my approach accordingly.

You'll gain insights like this from your audience too.

THINKING GLOBALLY

There's a big world out there. As an author, whether you like it or not, you are building an international publishing business. You should make it so that any reader anywhere in the world can purchase your books.

There is nothing wrong with exclusivity programs like Amazon's, but these programs are not good long-term strategies. You will lose all of your income if something happens to your Amazon account.

It is better to diversify your offerings by "going wide," which means distributing your book to as many places as possible so that more readers can buy them.

It also pays to diversify your formats—creating an e-book, trade paperback, and hardcover books, for starters. You should also consider audiobooks and large print where those formats make sense for your business.

It's true that many authors make more money in KDP Select than they make on other retailers combined, but this is a long-term game. It takes time to build audiences on other book retailers, and the sooner you start, the sooner you will future-proof your writing business.

Amazon uses algorithms to catch users that infringe on its rules. Sometimes, these algorithms catch innocent people in their crosshairs. Amazon takes a guilty-until-proven-innocent approach, and it's possible that your account could be canceled for reasons outside of your control. If that were to ever happen, it would be great to have a book business where readers can still buy your books.

Plus, it's just bad for business to depend on one source of income.

Amazon's exclusivity is mostly limited to the United States. The United States market is the largest book-buying market in the world, but it is not the only market. There are many readers around the world who cannot access Amazon, or who just don't like the company. By going exclusive, you prevent those readers from buying your books.

Therefore, aim to build a global publishing business by going wide.

MODELING AFTER THE PROS

The best way to learn marketing is to model the best-selling authors in your genre.

Pick four authors and study each one's marketing tactics for 90 days. You'll be surprised at what you learn when you go deep into an author's marketing practices. You'll see things that others miss. You'll also see missed opportunities.

If I were going to study an author's marketing, I would focus on their:

- Website
- Blogs/podcasts
- Social media channels
- Calls to action
- Lead magnets
- Newsletters
- Autoresponders
- Paid advertising
- Book covers
- Book descriptions
- Pricing

That's a good start. Become a student of that author.

Develop a dossier for every writer that you study. Over time, you'll notice commonalities. These commonalities are called table stakes, which are the minimum things you must do to be a player in your genre.

When you match table stakes and address missed opportunities that others are not taking advantage of, then you differentiate yourself in the market. If you do this correctly, it will become an advantage.

You may also discover that some authors do marketing tactics that make you uncomfortable. Remember what I said about marketing feeling good. Just because others are doing something doesn't mean that you have to.

Model yourself after the pros and you will become a pro. It's that simple.

THE MARKETING CREATIVITY
PROBLEM

Another common marketing problem is that authors struggle to be as creative in their marketing as they are in their books. Dreaming up new worlds and characters is no problem; sales copy for a book description? Oh, the agony!

There are tricks to help you quickly get into a creative mindset with marketing.

The first is a swipe file. It's what copywriters use for inspiration. It contains common marketing phrases, words, and examples of effective copy that they can use as a basis for their project. Many copywriters I know can't live without swipe files.

I have a swipe file that I add to whenever I encounter great copy in the wild. I frequently clip magazine, newspaper, social media, and book description sales copy. Sometimes the best copy ideas come from outside of publishing.

I have hundreds of examples that I can draw from when I need copy. That makes getting into a creative mindset much easier because I don't have to start from scratch.

The second creativity trick is to develop templates. If you have a successful book description, make that description the template for your next one. Or, use another author's book description as a template for your own (but please don't commit copyright infringement or plagiarism).

In any case, templates are a wonderful shortcut to help you build your marketing chops.

The third trick is to use tools. If there is a tool that can save you time, money, and effort, I suggest you strongly consider it.

For example, it's so 2012 to advertise one of your books on social media with just the book cover image. Most authors use attractive mockups with their book cover on a device such as an iPad for a physical book cover, usually against an attractive background with some copy. Until a few years ago, you had to have extensive Photoshop knowledge to build these mockups. Now, with tools like Canva and Book Brush, you can build these mockups quickly with little effort—and, most importantly, no design experience.

Having the right tools can be a godsend, especially if they're easy to use. If you shudder every time you open Photoshop, it will make creating marketing materials much harder.

To ensure the marketing muse shows up on demand, develop a swipe file, use templates, and adopt user-friendly tools. Your marketing skills will improve overnight, and you will get more consistent results. These tricks will also save you when you realize you must put something together at the last minute.

COPYWRITING

Copywriting is the art of writing text that compels customers to take action.

The text you write when you're copywriting is called copy. Examples of copy include book descriptions, email newsletters, autoresponders, and social media ads (like Facebook).

The actions that copy compels you to take include but are not limited to:

- buying a product
- clicking a link
- scrolling down a page
- watching a video
- joining a social media community
- sharing a post on social media
- and more.

There is no shortage of actions you can get readers to take. It depends on your goals and what you're marketing at the time.

Despite copywriting having "writing" in the title, it is a completely different skill set from fiction writing. This is why many authors find it difficult to write things like book descriptions and Facebook ads. Writing fiction versus writing copy is like speaking Spanish versus speaking Portuguese; it's similar, but it's not the same.

In fiction, we can be expressive, use language in interesting ways, and be as creative as we want.

We can also be creative with copywriting, but we must follow stricter rules.

Here are the copywriting rules I've learned over the years.

The first rule of copywriting is that copy should be short and punchy. The average person has an attention span of a goldfish. They will click away if you don't grab them with short, punchy copy. Long sentences and paragraphs no longer work.

I used to collect old magazines. *Time, LIFE,* and *National Geographic*. If you look at ads from the twentieth century, like in the 1960s and 1970s, it wasn't uncommon to see ads with paragraphs and paragraphs of text. This is an old-school style of marketing that is no longer in vogue. While long, narrative paragraphs used to be all the rage in the 1970s, you rarely see them today. Keep that in mind when you read some of the most recommended and praised books on copywriting, many of which are several decades old.

Today's copy has to be engineered for busy people with short attention spans.

The second rule of copywriting is that you should use plain language. Don't use anything higher than a fifth-grade vocabulary.

The third rule about copywriting is to avoid the passive voice. In his excellent book *Sales Copy for Fiction Writers*, Dean Wesley Smith talks about the importance of eliminating passive voice in your work. He argues that passive voice makes your copy dull, and it subconsciously pulls the reader out. He is absolutely right. Look at the sales copy for the world's largest companies like Apple, Microsoft, and Nike. You don't see any passive verbs *anywhere* in their marketing.

It's okay to use passive voice in your fiction, but rewrite it to make the verbs active when you're writing copy.

If you obey these three unwritten rules of copywriting, you will avoid many mistakes and minimize missed opportunities.

THE TRUTH ABOUT COPYWRITING

I wish I could give you a step-by-step guide to writing amazing copy, but the truth is that this is an acquired skill, just like learning to write engaging fiction.

Early in my career, I fell into the trap of leaving my book description for last. I'd cobble something together on the eve of publication, especially if the book was a sequel. Then I wondered why my books didn't sell.

Writing compelling sales copy boils down to the following tips:

- Study the world's best companies
- Study the world's best indie authors
- Use a swipe file
- Use a copywriting template based on your research
- Practice often
- Don't leave your copywriting to the last minute
- Spend a decent amount of time on your sales copy
- Give sequels just as much time as you would Book 1s
- Use an AI copywriting tool

How much time should you spend writing sales copy? I generally spend at least an hour on book descriptions. If I can spend several weeks writing a novel, I can spare an hour to write sales copy!

With shorter copy like Facebook ads, I work on the copy until I feel like I'm spending too much time on it. Once I have workable copy, I can usually feel it.

I also recommend checking out AI copywriting tools such as ChatGPT. They are quite good and will give you ideas you didn't consider. If you don't write copy often, they're worth the money. In fact, these tools may be able to write copy that's better than anything you could do yourself. They're excellent now, and the quality continues to improve rapidly.

The key is spending time on your sales copy and not treating it like an afterthought. If you do, you'll automatically sell more books.

CREATING GRAPHICS

Creating effective graphics is an essential part of most marketing tasks. Effective graphics are a must, whether you are designing a book cover, a Facebook ad, or nice graphics to use on your website.

Much like copywriting, designing graphics also makes many authors break into a cold sweat. After all, we are *writers*, not graphic designers. Most writers don't know one end of Photoshop from the other.

Fortunately, anyone can create attractive, eye-catching graphics. You just need to understand some frameworks and which tools you should use.

GRAPHIC DESIGN TEST PRACTICES FROM A NON-DESIGNER

Disclaimer: I am not a graphic designer, nor do I even attempt to claim I am good at it. At the beginning of my career, you could have described my graphic design skills as laughable. These days, they're so-so, but they are effective. I want to share some hard lessons I learned from designing terrible graphics.

First, I highly recommend taking some beginner graphic

design classes. You can find free courses online or cheap classes at your local community college. If you don't know the first thing about colors, composition, or typography, you owe it to yourself to learn from a professional. Otherwise, you will make ten times as many mistakes, and it will take you ten times as long to learn something as someone who devotes the time to learn the basics.

Next, remember that people read from left to right and top to bottom. If your design immediately draws people to the right side of an image, you are working against science.

Third, remember that certain elements draw your eye to an image. Pay close attention when you look at marketing graphics from now on. What is the first thing you see? Learn from that.

When you design an image, you have three jobs:

1. select the right image
2. select the right fonts
3. select the right colors

Get these things right, and design becomes much easier.

SELECTING THE RIGHT FONTS

Typography is everything. The difference between an amateur and a pro is their understanding of typography and fonts. I recommend reading the book *Thinking with Type* by Ellen Lupton. That book is a wonderful introduction to the world of fonts. You should also familiarize yourself with font sites like DaFont and Font Squirrel. These sites are font repositories. Though I don't recommend purchasing fonts from them (that's a topic for another book), I recommend you check out their font previewers. You can type in text and see what it will look like across dozens of fonts simultaneously.

You should also study font pairing. Some fonts go very well together. Others should not be caught dead in the same image. Also, pay attention to font pairings when you study marketing graphics. The simpler, the better.

SELECTING THE RIGHT COLORS

Color theory is important, but you can get lost in it. I recommend sticking to the most basic YouTube videos you can find on this topic. The important points to remember are that:

- the color wheel is your friend
- sometimes changing the color of the text can make all the difference in the world
- some images just don't look good with text laid over them, no matter what color you choose.

SELECTING THE RIGHT IMAGE

How do you find an effective image for your graphic?

Start with stock media. I recommend a *paid* stock media site.

I *do not* recommend using Creative Commons or any site offering free images for commercial use. This is because free sites and Creative Commons sites are frequently populated with stolen images that may look like you have the right to use them, but doing so would constitute copyright infringement. There are a lot of thieves out there.

You're not 100 percent guaranteed to be safe at a stock media photo site, but the chances of inadvertently committing copyright infringement are lower because these sites go to great lengths to police the quality of their content. Some sites even offer a liability guarantee if you purchase a photo that isn't what the creator says it is.

If you use anything other than vetted stock media, you do so at your own peril.

Stock media sites also have a wide variety of images likely to suit most of your marketing needs. It's easy to find almost any background you want as well as icons and illustrations. Stock media sites have affordable plans too, so they're not expensive. It would be a shame to get sued over an image that you could have just as easily paid a $15 license for.

Stock media sites also allow you to download sample images with watermarks so you can test them in your graphics. You only need to pay for the graphics that you use.

You'll find that many eye-popping graphics don't look so good when you put text on. The more you do this, the more you will get a sense of what works and what doesn't.

I also want to plug artificial intelligence art. Tools like MidJourney, DALL-e, and Stable Diffusion allow you to create stunning images by just typing in what you want. You can get illustrated, realistic, and even 3D models. The only limit is your imagination.

AI art has designers understandably worried, but I still recommend that authors consider it. These tools are the future. While the legal status of AI art is still questionable, there is no doubt that these tools can help you create compelling images too. Keep an eye on them, and don't discount them.

You should also beware of colorblind people. It's always a good idea to design colorblind-friendly graphics whenever possible.

YOUR AUTHOR WEBSITE: BEST PRACTICES

Every author needs a website. You could get by without one in the early 2010s. It was fashionable in some circles not to have a website.

Now, it's much rarer to encounter an author who doesn't have a website. If they do, at best, they're leaving money on the table. At worst, they're invisible.

It's more common nowadays to see bad author websites. I can't tell you how often I hear from authors who think they need to learn HTML to code their own websites. They think that a website built from the ground up *by them* is more sustainable. Wrong.

Your time is best spent writing, not coding websites. If you're a web developer by trade, then you're excused. But every time I've seen an author code their own website, *without exception*, each one looks like it was created in 1999. That's not a good look for readers coming to your website for the first time. Anything you do yourself is likely to be inferior to what you can get on the internet for free, especially with WordPress. Search engines will also be less friendly to your hand-coded website unless you know what you're doing.

Also, remember that website protocols change. Unless you're a developer by trade, it'll be impossible for you to keep up with all the security fixes you need to make. Amateur websites are vulnerable to hackers. WordPress is too, for that matter, but at least any themes you buy are created by professionals, so you're less likely to be victimized or targeted.

Websites don't cost very much. You can purchase an annual hosting plan and a domain name for less than $100 a year. If you plan on being a successful writer, you'll make far more than $100 a year in the long term. Your website is your calling card, so spend the $100 so you can make money versus being invisible.

This chapter contains the essential elements that every author's website should have.

A NICE AND CLEAN URL

I cannot overstate the importance of having a clean URL that is easy to say and spell. (Your author name should also be easy to say and spell too, but we won't go there.)

Readers will want to look you up if you're giving a podcast interview. If they can't spell your name, or if you use words in your URL that the average person can't spell, you're doing yourself a disservice.

Your URL should be professional too. Stay away from things like "authorname.WordPress.com." Keep your URL clean. Yes, that means you'll have to pay for one, but you'll look more professional.

HOME PAGE

This will be the most visited page on your website, and usually the place where all your visitors will start. At a minimum, I recommend including a photo, link, and brief description of your newest book and where to find it, and an email sign-up. Make sure the reader sees these things first.

ABOUT PAGE

The about page is the second-most visited page on your website. Tell your story and have fun with it. This page is your opportunity to connect with readers on an emotional level. They've probably just read one of your books and want to know about *you*, the author. Give them a compelling story and a reason why you should be their new favorite author.

Long about pages are fine as long as you break up the paragraphs so they're more readable. Include images, audio, and video if possible. I've used a short biographic video about myself for years on my about pages. You can view it at www.michael laronn.com/about or https://www.authorlevelup.com/about/. The friendly video sets the tone for the rest of my reader's visit. You can easily shoot a similar video on your cell phone in a well-lit room and edit it on Windows Movie Maker, iMovie, or even a free video editing app on your phone. Find a unique way to connect with visitors to your site.

BOOK PAGES

Book pages are relatively straightforward. There are two ways to do them.

The first method is the traditional way, which involves giving every book you write a dedicated page on your website. Include the book cover, book description, e-book or audiobook samples, and buy links.

The second method is the trendy way at the time of this writing that I think will probably go out of style, and that's to include covers, descriptions, and links to all your books on your home page. This way, your home page serves as a one-stop shop for readers. Honestly, this makes sense since the home page is the most visited page on your site, anyway. However, I think this trend will be short-lived because the more books you write, the more chance your home page will become cluttered. Also, you can't give out dedicated links to your book for your website, which every author will want to do at some point, especially when you have a bunch of books. If you're doing a podcast interview or a blog post, and you want to send people to your website to buy a book in your backlist, sending them to your home page is not a suitable option.

Again, this is my opinion, but if you have the time, I recommend dedicated pages on your website for all your books. Once you create them, let the books live there forever so you can drive traffic to those pages.

CONTACT PAGE

I've already ranted about contact pages, so I won't do that again here. But your website should have one *if* you want to connect with your fans. If you *do* have one, respond to your emails.

Contact pages can be tricky because plugins are the most common way to add them (on WordPress, at least). Sometimes those plugins get deprecated, and form submissions won't work, resulting in your fans' emails going into a black hole. Or, the form may stop appearing on your website. Be very careful here. Make it a point to test your contact form regularly. If you receive fan-mail regularly, but it stops suddenly, your contact form may not work properly. I learned that the hard way.

Here are my contact form best practices.

- Answer the most common questions readers might have about your website on the page directly above your contact form. This should cut down on the number of emails you receive. For example, if readers always ask you what the reading order of a series is, put that directly on your book page and tell people that on your contact form page.
- Always make sure the reader gets a confirmation. The confirmation should be easy to see. It can be on the same page as the contact form, or their submission could take them to a dedicated page that lets them know their message was received. Or, they could receive a confirmation email.
- Set time service expectations in your confirmation. Let the submitter know if it takes you a week to respond to emails.
- Ensure that your contact form works. Always test your forms!
- Ensure that you *receive* the emails. If your contact form goes directly to your spam filter, fix that immediately. Sometimes contact form emails come from weird email addresses; other times, they come directly from your email as if you were sending an email to yourself.
- Do your very best to respond to every email within the time service expectation you set in the confirmation.
- Check your contact page regularly to verify that it is still working. I recommend testing your page at least a couple times a year or when your normal contact form volume drops significantly.

PRESS PAGE

This page is optional, but it's a great addition for ambitious authors who want to secure blog, podcast, or video interviews. The press page sells your success and ability as a speaker. It might highlight your prior speaking engagements, your subject matter expertise, or even include videos of you speaking.

A good press page has two purposes:

- To attract press opportunities.
- To make it easier for the press to give you good press.

For example, on my press page, I highlight all of my speaking events—particularly that I've been a featured speaker on The Creative Penn, Mark Dawson's Self-Publishing Show, at Writer's Digest Conferences, and AnchorFM (now owned by Spotify). I also include videos of my most recent public appearances so the potential venues can see what I would be like as a speaker.

I also include a press kit, but we'll discuss that in the next chapter.

A press page is an important tool in your toolkit if you want to be a public speaker. My press page has made me a lot of money over the years and helped me grow my platform considerably.

If you'd like to view my press page in action, check it out at www.authorlevelup.com/press.

SITE NAVIGATION

You should also think about the top-level navigation of your website. Does it work? Is it logical? The simpler, the better, and the fewer pages, the better too.

I have seen some downright funky navigations over the years. People try to get cute with them, but I don't recommend that.

THE ULTIMATE AUTHOR WEBSITE

The ultimate author website doesn't exist, but you should still do your best. Resist the urge for perfectionism. Follow the techniques in this chapter, revisit your website every few months, and you'll find that it gets exponentially better over time.

Note that I did not include "design" in this chapter because you don't need a beautiful design. Some of the most effective websites I have seen look pretty terrible, but all the elements are there. You don't have to have the most beautiful website in the world—you just need to ensure that it's optimized for selling. Making it look nice is just a bonus.

YOUR EMAIL LIST

People have been saying that email is dead for years, but it is alive and well. I don't know anyone who doesn't rely on their email inbox to get things done. In fact, most people spend *too much* time in their email inboxes...but there's no guarantee that they'll receive *your* message. Spam filters are more powerful than ever, and there's no guarantee that all of your readers will see your emails anymore.

The techniques in this chapter have given me average open rates of 60 percent or higher, average click rates of 25 percent or higher, and unsubscribe rates under 1 percent. All of those numbers are generally considered to be above the industry average.

There is no accepted standard of what your open, click, and unsubscribe rates should be, but your open and click rates should be as high as possible, and your unsubscribe rate should be as low as possible. So, the techniques I use are effective, but they should only be a starting point for you. The best way to improve your email marketing stats is through deliberate trial, error, and experimentation.

As with all components of your platform, email marketing is

an art. While every author's email strategy will be different, there are clear ways to win at email marketing and clear ways to lose. Let's talk about how to lose first.

EMAIL FOR THE LOSE

Let's get one thing out of the way. **You cannot use your personal email address as an email service. No exceptions.**

If you use your Gmail or Yahoo account and place the email addresses of your subscribers in the blind carbon copy field, you will be blacklisted from your email provider and in violation of most countries' laws. These laws are clear in that a customer must opt in for email communications, meaning they must give you explicit permission to receive your emails. They must also be able to unsubscribe easily at any time.

When you email your subscribers with a personal email client and don't give them the ability to unsubscribe, it will piss them off. I have had the unfortunate displeasure of many authors adding my email to a blind carbon copy and sending me notices about their next books. When they do this, I can't unsubscribe without replying and telling them to take me off the list. Instead, because they need to learn this lesson the hard way, I mark their emails as spam and report them to their email service provider. This is unacceptable; if you do this, you will chase readers away and hurt your book sales. Readers don't forget this kind of thing. It shows them that you are unprofessional and can't be bothered to do your homework on email marketing best practices.

Here's another way to lose when email marketing: buying email lists.

Whatever you do, never, ever pay for email subscribers. It's unethical. These people didn't give you permission to email them, and they probably aren't interested in what you're selling because they don't know who you are. Buying an email list is one of the dumbest things you can do.

I also don't recommend participating in email marketing arrangements where readers sign up for one author's list, but their email is shared among multiple authors in that promotion. Readers should always know upfront if they are subscribed to someone's list. Imagine if they sign up for author A's email list, and then ten other authors email them with new releases. It's spammy.

And speaking of spam, here's another way to lose at email marketing: use subject lines that spammers often use.

Here's a quick exercise. Go to the spam folder in your current email address and see what words spammers use in the subject lines of their emails. Don't use those words. If spammers use them, then you should avoid them at all costs.

The final way to lose at email marketing is to email your subscribers too frequently. I have known aggressive internet marketers who will email you multiple times per day to buy a product, and if you don't buy, they will send you even more emails until you do. This is spammy, scammy, and unethical, even if it is a marketing best practice.

This is one of the reasons why internet marketers are bad role models for authors. They do things that may work in the short term, but they burn through customers and make it so that no one ever wants to do business with them again. Once this happens, they move on to another industry to find new pools of hapless customers.

Email marketing is a relationship business. Your subscribers have opted into your list because you wrote a book they liked, and they liked *you* enough to continue the relationship. Don't screw that up.

Think about it this way. If I met you one day and we became friends, would you appreciate it if I called you every day asking for money?

Of course not, so don't do it.

Again, I believe that internet marketers are bad role models in this area. Many of them are transient types and do not build long-term businesses. As an author, you are in the business of engaging with readers over the long-term.

Finally, let's talk about another way to lose at email marketing: bad copywriting. If you don't study copywriting, readers will unsubscribe from your list quickly. Readers expect emails to be short, punchy, and worth their time. If you want to sell them a book, sell them the book quickly. Don't take paragraphs upon paragraphs to get to the point.

As I wrote in the copywriting chapter, copywriting is not the same as fiction writing. It requires you to adopt a different mindset. If readers aren't opening your emails or taking the actions you want them to take, it is probably because of your copy.

THE TOOLS OF THE TRADE

To facilitate your email list, I recommend a reputable email marketing company like MailChimp, AWeber, GetResponse, or ConvertKit. These companies exist by the dozen and offer services that comply with every country worldwide. They allow your readers to opt in and unsubscribe from your list at any time, which are the two most important elements any email platform should have. Some email service providers offer free plans, but those plans usually come with limitations. Be prepared to pay a modest annual fee in exchange for email marketing services.

Another great thing about email marketing providers: you

own your email list and can take it with you when you leave. This isn't always true of other platforms such as social media sites.

Owning your list is key. You never know what could happen, so you want to ensure you can always communicate with your readers.

THE ANATOMY OF A GOOD EMAIL

Let's go through the steps you can follow to ensure that your newsletters and autoresponders convert as much as possible.

SUBJECT LINES

Subject lines are critical. Many marketers recommend spending more time on your subject line than the actual body of your email. I'm not so sure that is true for authors, but you should spend time crafting your subject line. Don't just throw it together.

The best way to craft good subject lines is to subscribe to as many mailing lists from authors in your genre as possible. Yes, that means you will receive more emails. I recommend using a burner email address to keep your primary email inbox clean. Signing up for other authors' mailing lists is free competitive intelligence and a missed opportunity if you are not doing it. (Yes, I recognize that this strategy does require you to take up space on someone's mailing list, but this is one of the best ways to find out what other authors in your genre are doing.)

You can also do a quick web search for blog posts that gather the most effective subject lines. Take the ones that jump out at you and put them in a file you can refer to when you need inspiration.

My trick is that I have over 200 potential subject lines to

draw inspiration from. It makes crafting subject lines so much easier.

Next, I recommend split testing subject lines if your email marketing service provider allows it. When you split test subject lines, the email marketing service provider will send the email with one subject line to roughly half of your audience, and the other subject line to the other half. It will then calculate a winner. Generally, you can only do this if your email list is over a certain size, but if you can, I always recommend split testing. It will eat into your results somewhat, but if you do it consistently over time, you'll get a sense of the subject lines that work best for your goals. For example, if you have a new book, you may want to test the subject line " New Release: [Book Title]" or

"[Book Title]: out now!" Or, you may want to try something completely different. Since new release newsletters will be the most frequent email you send, you owe it to yourself to determine the most effective subject line for this type of email.

AUDIENCE TARGETING

This aspect of email marketing is often forgotten.

Who on your email list are you sending your newsletter to? It sounds like an obvious question, but remember that your email list is not just a list of subscribers. It is a database of subscribers that meets certain parameters. For example, some subscribers are more engaged than others. Others prefer to read emails on desktop devices; some live in the United States, Canada, Australia, or another country. The bigger your email list gets, the more diverse it will become, and there may be situations where you don't want to send the same email to everybody.

The most common example is segmenting your email list into readers by retailer. When you have a new book launch, you send one email to Amazon subscribers, another to Kobo subscribers, and so on.

Here's another example of this, and one that can get you into trouble. If you have an autoresponder sequence, most people recommend *not* sending newsletters to subscribers currently receiving autoresponders. This is because you can overwhelm your subscribers with too many emails. If a subscriber receives an autoresponder on Monday and a newsletter on Tuesday, they're going to think you will email them every day. You don't want that. As we will discuss later in this chapter, you should only send your newsletters to subscribers who have completed your autoresponder sequence. This will keep things clean.

Depending on how you structure your newsletters, you may have additional parameters you want to filter your audience by. For example, if you write multiple genres (like horror and science fiction), you won't want to send new horror releases to your science fiction fans unless those releases have science fiction elements. Otherwise, your open, click, and unsubscribe rates will suffer.

My rule of thumb is this: send the right email to the right subscribers at the right time.

If there is even a remote chance that some of your subscribers won't be interested in the email you're sending, either think twice about sending the email or segment your list accordingly.

THE FIRST SENTENCE

If you have a subject line that compels readers to open your email, your first sentence is your next best opportunity to keep them interested. The first sentence is also generally what will appear in the preview section of their email client (if you don't specify separate preview text). I recommend telling the subscribers upfront what they're going to get in your first sentence so they know what's coming.

BODY

The body is...well, everything else. Your body text should be short and punchy. You should observe copywriting best practices. The best way to write body copy is to study others.

CALL TO ACTION

The call to action is anything you want subscribers to do once they reach the bottom of your email.

My biggest problem with call to actions was that I usually had more than one thing I wanted my subscribers to do. This is a no-no and usually works against you.

Be careful about giving your subscribers analysis paralysis. If you give them too many decisions, they won't make one.

Wherever and whenever possible, the best thing to do is to keep it simple. Every newsletter you send should have just one call to action. If there are multiple calls to action, just understand upfront that your subscribers will only take one of those actions, if they take one at all.

Next, what should your call to action look like? I don't think there is a wrong answer. Some people like to give plain links; others like to embed text with links (such as "Click Here"); others like to use colorful buttons or images as their call to action.

Again, I don't think there is a wrong answer. I recommend split testing to figure out what works best for you. Or, don't worry about it so much.

POSTSCRIPTS

A postscript function is similar to the postscript in a hand-written letter. You tell the subscriber something that you forgot to tell them in the body copy, or you tell them about something you want to especially draw their attention to.

Postscripts are effective because subscribers don't want to miss out. Postscripts catch your eye.

I've used postscripts to reiterate links I shared in the body copy, share some exciting and forthcoming news they can expect in the next newsletter, or give them something special, like a coupon.

I recommend postscripts, but I don't recommend going overboard with them. When used effectively, they train readers to read your emails all the way to the end, which is exactly what you want.

AUTORESPONDERS

An autoresponder is an automatic email that your email marketing service sends to an email subscriber when they take a certain action.

For example, you can set up an autoresponder that delivers a free book to a subscriber immediately when they sign up for your email list.

You can also set autoresponders to fire every week at the same time. You can send them for as long or as little as you want. This type of autoresponder gets readers up to speed with who you are and why you write.

Autoresponders have been so successful for me that I affectionately call them "my little salespeople." They are that effective.

Autoresponders are a way of life, and internet marketers use them in many ways to drive sales, engagement, and action.

No matter what you see someone do with autoresponders, you should keep yours simple. I have seen marketers develop autoresponder sequences that are hundreds of emails long. For example, when subscribers join a list, the marketer sends them a lead magnet. If the subscriber doesn't open the lead magnet within 24 hours, the marketer sends another email reminding them to open the lead magnet. On the next day, the subscriber receives another email promoting the marketer's course. If they click the link in that email and purchase the course, they will be moved into another sequence of emails that fires, giving them content from the course in a slow drip. If they do not sign up for the course, the marketer will harass them until they do, and if they *still* don't sign up, the marketer will remove them from the list.

I've oversimplified how many six- and seven-figure marketers use autoresponders, but my point is that you can go overboard. This level of complexity is not necessary for authors.

Instead, here's what works:

- Send the subscriber a lead magnet immediately when they sign up for your list.
- Follow-up in a couple of days to make sure that they got the lead magnet (because emails sometimes go to spam filters).
- The first week on the list, send them an autoresponder with a formal introduction to you and your work, with a link at the bottom to where they can find books on your website (or a link to your favorite social media profile, or other action you want them to take).
- During the third week, send them another email with more information about how you would like

them to engage with you.
- During the fourth week, do a harder (not too hard) sell of your most popular series.

That's a good start. For fiction, I think two to three weeks' worth of autoresponders is probably enough. For nonfiction, I would recommend going slightly longer, but just make sure that your emails are useful to the subscribers.

The autoresponders "warm up" your subscribers so that 1) you train them to open your emails and click your links and 2) they are ready to buy from you. Those are the only real reasons to use autoresponders.

Don't send an autoresponder without due diligence and care. You still have to follow the same rules that you would follow with a newsletter.

If you write and time your autoresponders properly, you'll find that your subscribers will be more engaged.

MANAGING YOUR LIST

Managing your email list is critical. Sometimes you will have subscribers on your list who stop opening your emails. They may not unsubscribe; instead, they will just delete or archive your emails. Therefore, they are taking up space and costing you money.

Every six months, I recommend pruning your email list. Use your email marketing services data to determine who is opening your emails, who is clicking on your links, and who is taking up space. Remove anyone who hasn't opened your emails in the past six months. This is called "list hygiene."

There are various methods to accomplish this. Some authors like to simply remove people who are not engaging with their content; others are more cautious about it.

Here's the problem: you don't really know how many people are opening your emails, despite what the email marketing service tells you. There are a few reasons for this. The first is that email marketing services track opens by using a pixel in your email. If this pixel is downloaded when the user opens the email, it counts as an open. However, some users prefer plain text email, and the pixel isn't downloaded in those situations. So, a subscriber could *appear* to not be opening your emails, but they could be quite engaged.

Another reason is that Apple now prevents email marketing services from seeing who opens emails on their devices using Apple Mail. This is a privacy feature that users can opt in for. When you consider how many people use Apple Mail daily, you can see the problem.

This is why some authors take a cautious approach when performing list hygiene. These authors identify a list of users who have not opened emails within a certain period. They then send these subscribers an email warning that they will remove them if they do not click a link at the bottom of the email (there are many variations on how they approach this). If the subscriber does not take the required action, then the author removes them from the list. This technique prevents accidentally removing an engaged subscriber from your list, which is a tragedy.

Whatever you do, just make sure that you maintain a healthy, engaged email list.

You may also learn more about your email subscribers over time and want to segment your list further based on that knowledge. For example, if you discover that a significant portion of your subscriber base lives in Australia, you may want to tag your Australian subscribers so that you can send them separate emails. Many situations like this can arise the bigger your email list gets.

YOUR BOOK ITSELF

Let's talk about using your books to sell more books. It's important to remember that the best marketing tool is almost always your next book. The more books you have, the more opportunities you have to reach readers.

Readers will be more likely to take a chance on you if you have more books. For example, if you write a series, readers may not buy the series until you have at least a few books published or have finished the series completely. This is because every reader has been burned by an author at least once. Authors quit mid-series all the time, and that's a terrible experience for readers. So is waiting years between series entries. Therefore, the more books you have in a series, the better.

Even if you write multiple series or stand-alones, I've never met an author who didn't benefit from more books. Yes, there is the problem of having so many books that readers don't know where to start, but I consider those good problems that can be easily solved with technology and basic marketing sense.

Don't let anyone talk you into writing fewer books for fear of overwhelming your readers. More books is always better. More books equal more choices for the readers.

Now that we've gotten that out of the way, let's talk about your book itself and why it is prime marketing real estate.

YOUR BOOK'S CONCEPT

What is your book about? Sometimes, people overlook this. Every book has a killer concept; you just have to figure out what it is. While it's true that some books can't be packaged no matter what you do, I don't believe that's true for most.

I believe it depends primarily on how well your book adheres to the high-level tropes of the genre and subgenre you're working in. For example, I write urban fantasy. Urban fantasy usually takes place in a city during contemporary times, and has magic, supernatural characters, and a fast pace. If I write a story that doesn't do any of those things and call it urban fantasy, I'm doing the book a disservice.

What often happens is that you'll write a book thinking that it will be one genre, but it will become something else, or a mashup. You'll start off with an idea of what you think the story will be, but then it becomes something else. When it's time to publish, you may struggle to determine which "box" to put it in. The answer to this problem is to know the genres you're working in and read widely in them. This creates more options for you because you will understand the genre on a deep level. If you write in different genres, this will be more difficult for you, but not impossible. Reading solves this problem, but it takes time and energy. You will learn where your book fits by reading more books in the genre and subgenre.

If you are struggling with where to place your book in the market, it is almost certainly because you haven't read enough books. If you have read many books and are still struggling with where to place yours, then it could be that you have something unique, but that's not a great situation to be in when you're marketing. Sometimes, you'll write books that are ahead of their time. Other times, you'll write books that you thought were marketable but actually belong in a different subgenre than you originally thought. So, the second solution to this problem is time. I know a lot of people don't like to hear that because they want to make money now, but the truth is that this is a long-term business. You will get better at writing and marketing the longer you do this.

FRONT MATTER

The front matter of your book is also prime real estate for promoting yourself and your other works. There are a few ways to do this.

The first is to use your copyright page strategically. On the page, put a simple link to your website where readers can learn more about you. This is a free tactic that takes just a few seconds.

The second way is to create a house ad. You could include a nice marketing graphic with all the covers in your series to let people know how many books they are in for.

The third way is adding testimonials, endorsements, or blurbs from other authors to build buzz for the book before the reader starts reading.

In any case, the only downside to using your front matter for marketing is that you want your readers to start reading the book as soon as possible. The downside to using your front matter for marketing is that for every page you take up, you will prevent the reader from jumping into your story. Front matter is prime real estate, but using it could come at the expense of shortening your sample.

That's why the back matter is a better option.

BACK MATTER

The back matter is a better place to promote your work because readers have finished reading, and they will expect some self-promotion.

After the last page of your story, you have a few options. All of them are equally viable and will depend on your audience.

1. Include a link to where they can buy the next book.
2. Include a sample of the next book (with a link to buy at the end).
3. Include a newsletter sign-up.

Remember that one call to action is almost always better than multiple.

Which should you choose?

There's no wrong answer. Just context.

If you want to keep things simple, then include sales copy for the next book, an image of the cover, and a link. This is the simplest method because it only takes up one or two pages, it's easy to create, and once you set it, you don't have to worry about it again as long as the link to the book on your website never changes. This method potentially leaves some money on the table, but I believe it is the best way to future-proof your books.

The next option is to include information about your book and a sample of the next book. This is a great idea because it's low friction. If readers like the book they just read, they can keep reading, and if they like the sample, they will almost certainly purchase it.

One problem with this method is that the second book may not be finished when you publish your first book. If so, you're going to have a problem. You will either need to wait until the next book in the series is done (so that you can include a sample), or you will need to go back and update your book later. This is problematic for many reasons, but the biggest problem is your paperback.

When you hire a designer to format a paperback, they have to use a certain template based on the number of pages in your book. If the page count of your book differs by more than ten pages, they will have to redo the sizing, which will cost you money.

If you're willing to put up with the juggling that this method requires, I believe including a sample can reduce the number of missed opportunities when readers arrive at the back of your book. Just know that you may not be able to do this with every book, depending on timing.

The final call to action type is a newsletter sign-up. Don't forget to inform your readers that you have a mailing list! Keep your copy simple and to the point.

There are some other alternatives you can put in your call to action, but I believe they are not as effective:

- asking for reviews
- asking people to follow you on various social media sites
- asking people to purchase a course, product, or service

First, I'm just not a fan of asking for reviews in the back of my books. I haven't done this in a long time. I believe getting readers to buy your next book is better than leaving a review. I also think that people are adults; if they like the book enough to review it, they'll review it. You don't need to twist their arm into doing so. But that's just me. But sure, asking for reviews can help in certain situations.

This is also obvious, but: make sure that the links in the back of your book are valid. Also, make sure that the user experience when the reader lands on your website is appropriate. You could consider creating "squeeze pages," which are pages on your site that do not have any navigation. The only option the reader has on these pages is to take the action that you require or leave. I used to use squeeze pages a lot, but I've migrated away from them because, like I said, I believe my readers are adults. If they want to click another link on my site because they're interested in it, I have no problem with that because all the pages on my site are optimized. But there is a time and place for squeeze pages—particularly if you are promoting a newsletter or a course.

YOUR BOOK COVER

You don't need me to tell you that book covers are an important marketing tool. That said, they are also the most difficult marketing tool to use correctly.

So many people think book covers are works of art, but that's not just what they are. Most covers *aren't* works of art. They are billboards.

Here's how a billboard works. You're driving along the highway, and you want something to eat. You see a billboard for a restaurant on exit 52, but you don't like that restaurant, so you keep driving, hoping you'll see something else in the next town. Before arriving at the next town, you spot a billboard advertising a restaurant you love. It tells you which exit and whether to turn left or right.

Book covers are the same way. Your readers are hungry for a certain genre, and your cover communicates to them whether the book will satisfy their hunger or not. Nothing more, nothing less. Thinking about your cover as a work of art is a fallacy because readers don't see the art when they're browsing. They only see the thumbnail of the book cover. So, in reality, it doesn't matter how intricate the details on your cover are or how beautiful it is—it only matters how eye-catching it is, and whether it conforms to readers' expectations of what a book cover in the genre and subgenre should look like.

If there is one thing I have seen in my decade-plus experience as an author, it is horrific book covers. They're everywhere. But what is most curious about some of these horrific covers is that they're effective.

One of the most memorable terrible covers I've seen is a best-selling self-published book that is apparently a thriller, and it has two dolphins swimming underwater. You can say a lot of things about thrillers; that they should have dolphins on the cover is not one of them. Yet, this book sells like crazy. It has garnered thousands of book reviews, and I suspect that it has allowed the author to make a comfortable living. Even more important, readers love it.

So, don't believe the hype about covers needing to be beautiful. There are some damned ugly covers that outsell beautiful covers every time.

Does that mean that your cover should be ugly? No, but I'm just trying to give you a dose of reality.

THE KEY QUESTION: SHOULD YOU DO YOUR OWN COVERS?

Before we discuss book covers for effective marketing, we must first discuss whether to hire a professional designer or do your book covers yourself.

Until a few years ago, I was firmly in the designer camp. I was terrible at Photoshop and didn't think I could ever design something effective.

These days, I design my covers. Are they beautiful? Probably not. Are they effective? Yes, because I understand what goes into a professional cover and have learned how to replicate it.

Both methods have pros and cons, and I think it ultimately boils down to what you are comfortable doing.

The pros to hiring a designer are:

- You will often get a higher quality product than if you designed the cover yourself.
- If you hire the right designer, they will be familiar with your genre and therefore offer ideas you wouldn't have considered.
- You don't have to spend nearly as much time; you just have to give direction designer.

The cons of hiring a professional designer are:

- It costs money.
- Everything depends on how well you communicate your idea to the designer.
- Just because you hire a professional does not mean you are guaranteed to get an amazing cover.

The pros of doing your own covers are:

- It is significantly cheaper.
- You own the copyright to the cover and can do whatever you want with it.
- You can change your covers faster, such as changing your print-on-demand page count.

The cons to designing your own cover are:

- The learning curve is substantial.

- Unless you're willing to put the time into learning design professionally, your results may be lacking.
- You will probably never be able to do the ultra-complicated techniques many professional designers use.

So, what should you do? I can't answer that question for you. You'll have to figure that out for yourself. But consider this: cover design is likely the most expensive cost in your publishing business. What would it mean if you reduced that cost by 70 or 80 percent? For starters, you would command a much higher profit. You can also use that money for other marketing tasks, therefore helping you grow your income further. Also, you won't be at the whim of designers raising their rates, which they do fairly often. I'll just leave that there for you to think about.

ANATOMY OF A COVER

A book cover consists of four different elements. When you understand the elements, you can put them together strategically to appeal to your target audience.

The Foreground. The foreground is the focal point of a cover. If a cover has a character on it, then the character is in the foreground. If there is a symbol or work on the cover instead, that is the foreground.

The Background. The background is everything behind the foreground. If a character is standing in a dark alley, then the alley is the background. The background is a great way to add subtle signals about the book's subgenre.

Author Name. The author name is self-explanatory. With your cover, you should make your author name the same on all your covers to improve your branding.

Book Title. The book title is also self-explanatory.

Series Title, Tagline, Or Endorsement. If your book is in a series, then you need to let readers know which book in the series it is. If your book is a stand-alone, you have a few other options. You can include a testimonial about the book from another author, a tagline that serves like a movie poster, teasing and hyping the book, or you could just list the genre of the book, like "A Novel" or "A Techno Thriller." The choice is up to you, but you should adhere to conventions in your genre.

Whether you hire a professional designer or design your own cover, you should keep these elements in mind. When hiring a designer, my best practice is to tell them what I want in each element. When I do my own covers, I intuitively know what needs to be in the design.

Let's take our understanding of the different elements further by using some working examples.

What Signals is Your Cover Giving Off?

A book cover is a series of signals. While the art may be pretty, more important is whether the signals are speaking to your target audience.

We are going to use two working examples in this chapter:
- steampunk fantasy with dragons
- a sweet contemporary romance set in a small town

The Foreground

.   .   .

The first element is the foreground, which contains the main focal point: the characters or important symbols on the cover. This is usually what the reader sees first, so you want to make sure that the centerpiece of your cover instantly screams the book's genre and subgenre.

For our steampunk fantasy with dragons, you would want a character that says steampunk. This means historical clothes, accessories such as goggles, antiquated inventions, or even prosthetics. If the character uses magic, you want magical elements prominent. A dragon would also be helpful, either in the foreground or background.

You would want a couple in the foreground for the sweet contemporary romance set in a small town. Clothing choices that indicate small towns might include flannel, jeans, cowboy hats, and so on. Since the story is a sweet romance, the couple's pose should be innocent. Maybe they're holding hands, or if it's a male/female story, the female is resting her head on the male's shoulder.

The Background

The background is everything behind the foreground, and in my opinion, it is underrated. You can put many reader signals in the cover's background.

For our steampunk example, does the story take place in a major city? The Wild West? Small town? What country? What period? Don't underutilize your background.

For our sweet romance, we would want something that indicates a small town: a farm, a town square, a market, a rustic home, a cottage, and so on.

. . .

Title and Subtitle

The book's title is also an important signal. The font you choose and the typography effects are everything. At a minimum, they should match other books in your subgenre.

For our steampunk fantasy, we would want a common fantasy font with magical effects around it. We might also want it to look like steampunk, such as including gears in the typeface.

For our romance, we would want a romantic font, possibly with flourishes or cursive letters.

Author Name

Don't forget about your author name. You should follow the same rules as your title and subtitle, but you'll also want to make it stand out. Your author name is a great opportunity to establish branding on your cover too.

Putting It All Together

Let's look at the reader signals that compile our covers.

For our steampunk fantasy, we might have a cover with the following elements:

•female heroine on the cover wearing Victorian clothing and goggles, with a prosthetic arm covered in swirling magic

•airship and dragons in the background, flying high over the London skyline

•the book title in gold letters with embellishments that make some letters look like cogs

•the author title in a similar dramatic font

For our contemporary sweet romance, we might have a cover with the following elements:

•a couple holding hands and smiling

•a main street background, with a modern pickup truck parked on the street

•the book title is a cursive, romantic font

•the author name in big letters to establish the romance author's brand

Think of your book cover as an ecosystem. Every element has its part, but everything works together to sell your book.

This is helpful when you're ordering a cover. Outline the different elements for your designer and tell them what you want.

When you're working with your designer and the design doesn't look good, isolate the elements to figure out what isn't working so you can communicate that clearly to the designer.

I hope that now you'll never see book covers the same again.

THE IMPORTANCE OF DOING YOUR HOMEWORK

You should be an expert in covers in your genre. You should keep a library of best-selling covers on your desktop or on a site like Pinterest so that you can refer to them often.

I keep a dossier of best-selling covers organized by certain parameters on my computer. For example, I write urban fantasy, which is gender-driven and has many subgenres. This way, if I ever want to design a book cover in a certain subgenre, I can simply pull out my reference covers for inspiration. It works wonders.

However you do it, research is a must. Your chances of landing an effective cover will depend on how adept you are in your knowledge of your genre and subgenre, and how well you can communicate your desires to the designer.

WORKING WITH A DESIGNER

There are tricks you can use to improve your communication with your designer.

I have made many mistakes when hiring cover designers. If I can save you from at least a few of them, then this book will have paid for itself.

First, instead of conveying your book's content to your designer, focus on conveying the genre and subgenre instead. Resist the default urge to tell the designer all about your book. I hate to tell you this, but they won't care. What they will care about, however, is where the book will fit in the market. Your job is to help the designer understand this market fit.

When you think about designing covers like this, then you realize that your job is to provide clarity to your cover designer.

In 2014, I hired a designer to do a cover for my *Moderation Online* series, which is a science fiction story about a gang of terrorist vegetables trying to take down an empire of evil processed foods. No matter how you spin it, the story is one hell of an idea, and quite difficult to convey on a cover.

I made some critical mistakes when I filled out the designer's brief. First, I told him everything that happened in the story. Second, I didn't understand the genre or subgenre. Third, I gave the designer too much information.

The result was that the designer sent me a well-illustrated

design, but he was confused about the genre. It wasn't the designer's fault. It was *my* fault because I didn't give him clarity.

You will get a confused cover design when you give your designer too much or too little information. Therefore, you must provide clarity.

Here's how to provide clarity:

- Send the designer reference covers that look like what you're going for. Those reference covers should be in the subgenre you're writing in.
- Use bullet points. Seriously. Don't overwhelm your designer with paragraphs upon paragraphs of information. Give them short and succinct bullet points. They will thank you for it, and you will receive a better design.
- When you receive a cover draft, provide your feedback and bullet points separated by the four elements of the book cover. Isolate your feedback to each element. This will improve your communication with the designer considerably.

Follow those tips, and you'll find that your designers have more clarity. You'll also increase your chances of receiving a professional, *effective* cover that speaks to your target audience.

MORE PRO TIPS ON COVER DESIGN

Here are some other miscellaneous tips that have helped me tremendously over the years when working with a designer:

- When you receive the first draft of the cover and don't like it, take a deep breath, go on a walk, and don't reply to the email immediately. Reflect on why you don't like the cover. This will take the emotion out of your feedback.

- Often, it's usually one or two elements on the cover that you don't like, not the entire cover. When you fix those elements, the cover can become exponentially better. Sometimes, knowing what to fix is superior to starting over.

- It's never the designer's fault if you have an ugly cover. It is *your* fault. As the author, the responsibility starts and ends with you.

- When you receive a cover draft, always put it next to your other reference covers. If you use Pinterest, put it on your Pinterest board. This will help you determine if your designer hit a home run or if they have work to do. Then, send your cover image next to the reference covers so they can see what went wrong.

- If something isn't working, it is better to tell the designer to start over, but you should do that early. Don't be the author who goes through five drafts, only to start over. That will frustrate your designer and reduce the quality of your design because they will want to get rid of you.

- When designing, inspect every little detail. And I mean *every little detail*. Assuming you hired the right designer, they will still make mistakes. For example, I had a designer who provided a trilogy of covers for me. Book 1's cover was amazing. When they sent me Book 2's cover, I discovered that the author name was a few centimeters higher than the author name on Book 1. When I switched between them, it was painfully obvious. As another example, I once went several years between books in a series, and the designer forgot that they did something special for me on the spine of the paperback. The result was mismatched spines. This is the sort of thing that your designer should automatically check, but it can sometimes fall through the cracks because designers are busy. Therefore, you must police every single detail of your cover.

- This won't help you with marketing, but remember that unless you sign a contract that indicates otherwise, the designer owns the copyright to the book cover. This means that the designer is licensing the cover to you for commercial use. This also means that the designer would be within their rights to revoke their license at any time...unless you signed a contract that says otherwise.

- If you sign a contract that transfers the design's copyright to you, not so fast. In the United States, there is a legal principle called "copyright termination," which allows authors and artists to get the copyrights to their works back even when they sign a contract giving them away. The intent behind copyright termination is to protect artists who sign bad contracts early in their careers. This means that 35 years after the contract, the designer can take back the copyright to the cover. Now, is it likely that your book cover will be the same for 35 years? No, but you're still taking that risk. There are clauses you can insert into your contract to minimize this risk, but that requires the counsel of an experienced attorney.

BOOK DESCRIPTION

Your book description is also vitally important. Once the cover attracts your reader and they click on your book, your book description will help them determine if they should buy.

Since we just dissected book covers, why not do the same with book descriptions? We can break them down in a similar way. When you understand the components of a book description, you can write a more effective description.

Let's re-use our working examples:

- steampunk fantasy with dragons
- a sweet contemporary romance set in a small town

THE HEADLINE

If you can only spend an hour writing a book description, spend most of it on your headline. Good headlines sell books. The best part about the headline is that if it doesn't work, you can change it—and it costs you nothing.

Here's a formula for an effective headline: character + genre signal + problem + intrigue.

With our steampunk fantasy example, here's a headline: "Luna boarded the seven o'clock train for Savannah, Georgia, to visit her uncle for the summer. Too bad the train was a dragon in disguise."

With our sweet romance example, here's another: "When Pam moved back to her hometown to save her family farm, the last thing she thought about was love."

Be creative with your headlines, but not clever. Remember that your headline is a signal; pack as many signals to your target audience into it as you can.

THE FIRST PARAGRAPH

If the headline is the most important part of the book description, the first paragraph is the second-most important part. It serves as a follow-up to the tone and content you established in your headline.

With our steampunk fantasy example, you might talk about how Luna is an inventor whose inventions never quite work right, and how her uncle, a local businessman with no patience for science, automatically doesn't like her endeavors.

With our sweet romance example, you might talk about how Pam is a successful businesswoman returning to the town where she grew up, and all her friends were nearly as successful as her.

In any case, this is your opportunity to give the reader a first impression of your character and the story.

THE BODY

I like to think about everything after the first paragraph as "everything else." It's important, but not nearly as important as the headline and first paragraph. If you don't get those two right, the rest of the book description won't matter.

To get the body right, you want to describe the stakes, the villain, or anything else that a prospective reader needs to know. The trap is summarizing your story; best-selling writers don't do that. Therefore, it pays to learn copywriting and to emulate what the bestsellers in your genre are doing.

THE CALL TO ACTION

Don't forget to end the book description with a call to action. It's just good salesmanship. Ask your readers to buy the book and find a way to make the sentence sizzle.

Whatever you do, don't wait until the last minute to write your book description. Spend some time on it, give it the attention it deserves, and you'll find that you'll make more sales.

BOOK RETAILER SALES PAGES

Each retailer is different. Yet, you should follow some best practices so that your books look good on all retailer sales pages.

This chapter covers best practices. This chapter does not go into any specific retailer; rather, you should be able to apply the advice at most if not all retailers.

PRICING

The principles of book pricing are simple.

First, assuming you are a self-published author, you must price your books to receive the highest royalty tier possible. Note that I didn't say the highest royalty. On some retailers, how you price your book will affect how much you earn. On Amazon, in particular, at the time of this writing, books priced between $2.99 and $9.99 receive a 70 percent royalty. Books priced below $2.99 and above $9.99 only receive a 35 percent royalty. Which would you rather have?

Next, you must price your book in line with other books in your genre. This means you would be idiotic to charge $14.99 for an e-book. You would also be idiotic to charge $0.99 for all of your novels 365 days a year. You must do competitive research to determine what other authors are charging and then do that.

While we're discussing comparative pricing, you should also charge less than traditional publishers. Traditional publishers charge more money because they have more overhead. They have staff, vendors, and other suppliers that they must pay to produce their books. You do not. I have met authors who insist on charging $9.99 for everything they write. These authors are leaving money on the table.

Next, you must determine a pricing strategy for your series. Some authors price the first books in a series cheaper to entice readers to take a chance on it. Some authors go even further and make Book 1's "permafree," which means that it is permanently free. I don't think either of these is a bad strategy; you just have to be intentional about it.

Next, you must also price your book correctly for each format. I already discussed e-book pricing earlier. For trade paperback pricing, you must price your book to be attractive to bookstores. This means also giving it a sufficient discount, usually 55 percent. For audiobooks, assuming you aren't exclusive to Audible, you'll have to do research to figure out what other authors in your genre are charging, but my experience is that you will have more latitude. Audible has a near-monopoly on the audiobook industry and automatically prices its books based on length. I think that's a bad idea, but there's nothing we can do about it. Other audiobook distributors such as Findaway Voices and Author's Republic distribute to retailers outside of Audible and do not place this pricing restriction on their authors. The problem at the time of this writing, in my experience, is that most authors who produce audiobooks are exclusive to Audible, so there is a dearth of independent and "wide audiobooks." As a result, it's not always clear how you should price your books. I have found that the pricing strategies of other authors are quite scattered and inconsistent. So, for the foreseeable future, until Audible's stranglehold is broken, you're on your own with audiobook pricing.

Next, you must also price your book correctly by country. This is harder than it sounds. For example, in the decade-plus I have been publishing, I have yet to see a definitive resource that explains what you should charge in each currency. Exchange rates fluctuate.

For example, in 2014, I would have told Americans to price their books higher in euros because they would have benefited from strong exchange rates. In 2022, the euro is now 1:1 with the dollar, and the exchange rates aren't so strong. Also, an American's pricing strategy would inevitably be different from a Brit's or Aussie's, since exchange rates differ between currencies. As I said, this can be maddening, and once you dig deep into it, you see just how complicated pricing really is.

You will have to research how authors in your genre are pricing their books in foreign currencies. In my experience, you will probably find that there is no consistency. That's okay; this can become a market advantage for you.

I consider the major world currencies to be the Australian dollar, the British pound, the Canadian dollar, the euro, and the United States dollar. The other currencies are nice, but they represent smaller markets. Establish a currency strategy for each currency and be consistent with it across all retailers. When you do that, your book pricing will look more attractive to local readers, and they will be more likely to buy your books if they are priced correctly and attractively. In other words, make it look like you've done your homework. If you don't know what to charge, make your best guess.

Also, when doing currency research, avoid using traditional publishers as your comparisons at all costs. Remember that their overhead is significantly higher. I believe that traditional publishers are overpricing their books in foreign currencies. Combine that with the fact that book retailer currency converters result in astronomically high prices, and you have unaffordable books. That's not what you want.

When you develop a pricing strategy, I recommend that you write it down so that you can make all of your books consistent. Every time you publish a new book, pull out your currency list. This will ensure that you do it consistently every time.

Pricing is an art, not a science, and you should be prepared to adjust your strategy accordingly. Also, remember that the more books you have, the more cumbersome it becomes to adjust your strategy quickly.

METADATA

Book retailers also allow you to customize the metadata for your book to aid discoverability. Metadata is information about your book that describes the book, and it tells retailers where to put it on their shelves.

Common examples of metadata include your book's title, subtitle, author name, series name, and series number.

Wherever possible, hinting at the subgenre in your title and series title is always a good idea. This just makes everything easier from a marketing perspective.

Other examples of metadata include categories and keywords.

A category is like a digital bookshelf. Examples include fantasy, urban fantasy, epic fantasy, and so on. There is a big difference between the aforementioned genres.

Every retailer that I know of adheres to the Book Industry Standards and Communications ("BISAC") classification system, which is the industry standard for categorizing books. I don't find BISAC useful because it doesn't go granular enough. For example, I write urban fantasy, which is a universe of subgenres and styles. BISAC classifications don't capture these nuanced details, but it is what it is.

If you have a straightforward book with a clear genre and subgenre, then you should have no problem finding the right BISAC classifications. The trouble comes when you have a mashup book that doesn't fit neatly within a category. If that happens, just do the best you can.

Another important metadata item is keywords. Retailers also allow you to enter a certain number of keywords that describe the book in greater detail. In the example of urban fantasy, your keywords might include werewolves, magic, and the name of the city where your series takes place, for starters.

Keywords are helpful but not as effective as they used to be. When I started in 2012, you could launch a career if you picked the right keywords and had the right book with the right timing. Now, that is no longer true.

There are great tools to help you do advanced keyword research if you need them. You will have to research the right keywords for your book. You can always change them if needed. Just know that the success of your book probably won't be because you picked amazing keywords. Keywords can only help you so much.

ADDITIONAL PRODUCT PAGE ITEMS

Each retailer offers different tools to help you improve your sales. Amazon offers an Editorial Review section, A+ content, and an Author Central profile, to name a few. Kobo offers a promotions tab to help you promote your titles. Retailers are always changing their tools and adding new ones, so I recommend becoming a student of each retailer's methods and weaving those into your marketing and promotion strategies.

REVIEWS

Ah, reviews. They are the toughest thing to get when you are a new author.

I used to agonize over reviews until I realized that, for the most part, they were outside of my control. The difficulty with obtaining them is that you have to hit the right readers at the right time with the right book. That is amazingly difficult. It's especially difficult if you are a new author with no clout or momentum.

In this chapter, I will review a few common ways to obtain reviews, but just understand that nothing is guaranteed. Don't be discouraged if it takes a while to get reviews. Almost all of us have to fight this good fight too.

GETTING TRADE REVIEWS

I wrote earlier that you should never, ever pay for reviews. There is one exception: trade reviews.

If you want to pursue a trade review, you should only pursue ones from reputable sources, and even then, you should have a clear strategy.

The best reason to purchase trade reviews is when selling to bookstores or libraries is a cornerstone of your marketing strategy. When I say cornerstone, I mean that you want to aggressively pursue bookstores. Unless you're doing that, I don't think trade reviews are worth it. They are expensive, and the only people who were going to read them are bookstores and traditional media outlets. Typical readers don't care one iota if *Publishers Weekly* or *Kirkus* reviews your book.

If you pursue trade reviews, do so with clear eyes. You may not get any, and the reviewer may not like your book. That's just how it goes. But, if you target bookstores or libraries, trade reviews are a great way to compel them to buy.

ASKING YOUR EXISTING AUDIENCE

If you have readers, don't be afraid to ask them for reviews. You can use your newsletter, and social media channels, or even ask readers who send you fan-mail. I'm not a huge fan of this method because, as I said, I believe adults are adults, and if they wanted to leave you a review, they would have. As long as you don't come off as too desperate, I believe a writer's gotta do what a writer's gotta do. As you become more successful, just know that you don't have to keep doing it.

Another way to obtain reviews is to look for book bloggers. There are hundreds of book bloggers who review indie books. There are also plenty of directories you can find with websites and email addresses. I won't name any because these resources go out of date quickly, but you can find them with a simple web search for "book bloggers plus [insert your genre]."

Reaching out to book bloggers is a numbers game. I don't want you to think that every book blogger you reach out to will review your book. Most won't.

Here is my experience. If I reach out to one hundred book bloggers, I can expect roughly 25 to respond saying that they are interested (if I'm lucky—sometimes 25 is optimistic). Out of those 25 that are interested, I can expect about five to leave a review. To keep the math simple, I would expect about a 5 percent acceptance rate, and that is if you have an amazing book with a killer cover, killer book description, and marketing potential. As you can see, those numbers aren't so good. Some authors will do better than others; I have sometimes seen review rates of ten to twenty percent, but that's rare. Your mileage will vary, but I would keep your expectations on the low side.

This is a numbers game. The more people you reach out to, the higher the probability of receiving a review, but you have to weigh the effort required with the reward. Is it worth your time to spend hours and hours emailing people who will never email you back? It is, but only up to a certain point. Also, I don't recommend reaching out to book bloggers who are not in your genre. That is a colossal waste of time.

There are also book review services where you can pay a small fee to have your book listed on a website where avid readers can download it. You only pay when they download the book. Examples include Book Sirens and Book Sprout.

Let's get one thing straight: never, ever pay for reviews. It is unethical, and it is cheating. It will also get you banned from retailers and expelled from polite society among writers.

When I first started publishing, there was a certain writer who shall not be named who became infamous for paying for reviews. The backlash against this person was swift. The sad part was that he was a great writer. Don't let that happen to you. Never pay for reviews, no matter how tempting it may be. You will be found out.

HOW TO ASK FOR REVIEWS

Okay, so you have decided on the best way to get reviews. How do you go about it?

To start, you must have a good cover, book description, and book. This means having a professional cover, professional editing, and good storytelling ability.

Next, you need to make it easy for readers to leave reviews for your book. Easy means a link that takes the reader to the review entry page for your book on various retailer sites. You can create these links with tools like Reader Links or Genius Link.

Make it easy. All readers should have to do is click the link, type in their review, and be done. If you can do that, you're doing it correctly.

DISTRIBUTION

This chapter will cover some marketing decisions you need to make to distribute your books. Distribution means how and where you sell your books. As I discussed in previous chapters, I recommend "going wide," which means selling your books at as many places as possible so that readers anywhere in the world can buy your books at any time. This is an excellent long-term business strategy for any author.

Let's talk about distribution strategies by format.

E-BOOK DISTRIBUTION

E-book distribution is the most straightforward distribution to understand. I recommend creating an account at any retailer that allows you to do so, and using a distributor like Draft2Digital to sell your books to smaller retailers that you couldn't reach otherwise.

You will always be better off selling books directly through a retailer because you will net a higher royalty. The only downside is that the wide lifestyle is often death by dashboards. You will have to manage many dashboards, which can be a turnoff for some people. But it's usually worth it.

As I recommended in a previous chapter, become a student of each retailer. Learn how they structure their metadata and what tools they have for marketing. Each retailer is different, and they change their standards often.

PAPERBACK DISTRIBUTION

When I refer to "paperback" in this chapter, I refer to trade paperbacks, hardcovers, and large print titles.

Paperback titles are also a critical format for authors. At the time of this writing, you have two options: distribution with a free ISBN and distribution with a paid ISBN.

ISBN stands for International Standard Book Number. I always recommend that authors purchase ISBNs with their publishing business as the publisher of record. Depending on your country, your government may provide ISBNs for free, but most authors have to pay for them.

ISBNs are expensive but worth it. I recommend that you only purchase ISBNs through the licensed agency in your country that is permitted to sell them. Otherwise, your publishing company name may not be listed as the publisher of record. I do not recommend purchasing ISBNs directly through a retailer.

When you have an ISBN that you own, you can distribute your books through Ingram, the world's largest print distributor. Bookstores use Ingram for distribution and fulfillment, so if your book is in the Ingram catalog, bookstores can buy it. (This doesn't mean that they *will* buy it; it just means that they *can* if readers ask for it.)

Many bookstores don't like Amazon, and rightfully so. If you use KDP Print to distribute your books, then bookstores also won't buy them because they won't be able to purchase the book with a good discount. In other words, only distributing your books through KDP Print means that paperback buyers will only be able to purchase your book on Amazon, thus limiting your distribution. This is why I recommend purchasing your own ISBNs. At first, it seems like this is a waste of money because if you are an unknown author, you probably won't see many sales through Ingram. Remember that this is a long game and that little income streams significantly increase over time. My focus would be less on maximizing your book sales *now* than building a foundation upon which your book sales can *explode* if you ever get that lightning strike. Optimizing your books for Ingram and bookstores is just good marketing.

I also want to address large print editions. I love large print editions because certain readers prefer paperback titles but need the text to be bigger.

That said, there is a time and a place for large print editions. Some readers prefer them; some do not; in my experience, it depends entirely on the genre. I think readers will favor large print editions more as they age, so even if this format is not customary in your genre now, it could be several decades later. You may want to consider this in your marketing strategy. In my mind, it never hurts to have more formats available for your book as long as they are easy to create and easy to buy.

AUDIOBOOK DISTRIBUTION

Audiobook distribution is tricky. For a long time, Audible (owned by Amazon) had a monopoly on the audiobook market, at least in the United States. Now that seems to be changing with the introduction of new players like Findaway Voices (owned by Spotify) and Author's Republic, who specialize in distributing audiobooks to readers outside of the United States. As a result, the audiobook market is heating up.

However, for over a decade, Audible had a good head start. It locked authors into exclusivity arrangements by limiting the royalties they can earn. You earn 40 percent of each sale if you are exclusive to Audible. If you engage in a royalty share with a narrator, then you only earn 20 percent (and your book must be exclusive with Audible). If you are not exclusive, then you only earn 25 percent. Is your head spinning yet?

We need to talk about Audible distribution because it determines everything else you do with your audiobooks.

First, I do not recommend going exclusive to Audible. I did this earlier in my career, and it was a mistake.

Next, I also do not recommend engaging in royalty shares with narrators. Most authors do not read the fine print when signing Audible's royalty share agreement, but if they did, they would realize that it is in perpetuity. Most authors understand that Audible's exclusivity lasts for seven years, but they do not know that the perpetuity clause of a royalty share agreement overrides the exclusivity agreement. If you want to escape the perpetuity of a royalty share agreement, you must buy out your narrator. Not only is this expensive, but you'll also lose all of your reviews.

So don't do what I did. I had to buy out my narrators for all of my early audiobook projects, and it cost me a substantial amount of money. If you can't afford to produce an audiobook, then don't produce an audiobook. Don't let Audible's nice marketing copy cloud your thinking, because there are legal ramifications.

Now that we've gotten Audible distribution out of the way, let's talk about wider distribution. I still recommend that you publish your books through Audible; just make your distribution non-exclusive. Many websites want high-quality audiobooks, including Overdrive and Audiobooks.com. The readership on these sites is substantial, and you'll never be able to reach them if your books are only available on Audible.

AI AUDIOBOOKS

You should also consider creating artificial intelligence audiobooks. The format is still nascent at this time, but it is growing in popularity. In 2022, Google Play opened the beta for its auto-narrated audiobook program to any authors publishing on its platform. With just the click of a button, you can create an audiobook whose narration is almost as lifelike and expressive as a human-narrated book (for nonfiction). You can create this audiobook and offer it at a lower cost than you would a human-narrated audiobook. This is a great alternative and supplement to human-narrated audio.

Naturally, this format has narrators more than a little nervous, but I believe that AI audio can and should coexist with human-narrated audio. There are just some books that don't make sense to hire a human to narrate. For example, I produce a quarterly book series called *Indie Author Confidential*, which recaps the lessons I am learning in my journey to become a successful writer. It makes zero sense to hire a narrator *every* quarter to read these books. It also makes zero sense for me to narrate them myself because it would be time-consuming. AI audio is an excellent fit for this series.

DIRECT SALES

I also recommend selling your books directly to readers. Selling e-books and audiobooks directly is easy, thanks to tools like Book Funnel, but selling paperbacks directly is still tricky at this time. There are tools, but you'll have to pay for them and weigh whether you want to bear the time, energy, and costs of direct shipping. I've done the calculus myself and have determined it's not worth it until I am more successful and readers start asking for it. You'll have to make this decision for yourself.

If you're not selling your books directly to readers, then you're leaving money on the table. The key when selling books direct is to make it easy. It must be:

- easy to buy
- easy to troubleshoot when the reader has problems
- easy to sideload onto readers' devices

Tools like Book Funnel and Story Origin accomplish all three of these goals. Otherwise, you will have to do your own customer service and fulfillment with readers, and you don't have time for that.

LIBRARIES

Getting your books into libraries is great but requires a lot of work. At a minimum, I recommend making your book available for libraries to purchase. After that, it's up to you how much more work you want to do.

To make your book available for libraries to purchase, I recommend distributing your books through Baker & Taylor and Draft2Digital. This will ensure that your e-books can be purchased and priced for libraries accordingly.

You can be more aggressive in reaching out to libraries if you want. For example, there are resources you can find in the indie community that teach you how to reach out to the acquisitions librarian who purchases titles. If you want to go this route, there are special ways to do it, and I recommend using these resources to do so.

You can also donate your books to libraries. Generally, libraries don't put donations on their shelves, but they will sell them instead. This is still critical visibility as many people visit library sales.

Lastly, if you want your books in libraries, ask your readers to ask their local librarian. Ultimately, libraries purchase books their patrons want. Consider reminding readers to ask for your books at their local library if they want to support you.

In any case, libraries have not been a big part of my overall strategy, but I do sell quite a few audiobooks to libraries through Findaway Voices. This is why making your book *available* is key.

RETAIL SHOPS

By retail shops, I refer to gift shops and other retail stores that don't specialize in selling books, but may offer books in their product offering.

This distribution channel is not for everyone. I once spoke to a children's book author who wrote Christmas books that she sold almost exclusively to gift shops in her region. She would put books in her trunk, drive to every retail shop she could find, and she would promote the book. More often than not, the stores purchased the book because there was a healthy contingency of moms who were always looking for books to buy for their children. This author made over six figures per year in paperback sales to these stores, which is jaw-dropping. Even more jaw-dropping is that, when I first spoke to this author, she had no idea about the modern methods of using e-books and print-on-demand retail sites.

That's the power of retail shops, but they're not suitable for every genre.

LITTLE FREE LIBRARIES AND OTHER FREE LIBRARIES

I don't know if this is true everywhere, but over the last decade, I have seen a proliferation of Little Free Libraries, which are simple wooden shelves that people build in their front yards that house books. Passersby can see what's in the library, take a book, and even leave a book.

In my neighborhood, Little Free Libraries are on every corner. You can bet that I leave my books in these libraries. Why not?

While writing this chapter, I did a quick web search and discovered 25 Little Free Libraries in my zip code alone.

Another free library you should consider is the library at your local hotel or coffee shop. They frequently have shelves where you can grab free books from and leave books as well. Leave a copy of your book on the shelf before you check out from the hotel. Even better, autograph it!

But, you really, really, *really* need to make sure that you have a great cover that looks professional and would fit in with other books in your genre. Otherwise, no one will touch your book, and the staff will probably throw it out.

You can also find these free libraries in your local coffee shops and other small business establishments, so don't disregard them.

EMAIL NEWSLETTER PROMOTION SERVICES

There is one technique that has been around forever, and it doesn't appear to be going away anytime soon: email newsletter promotion services. The most famous of these services is BookBub.

These services aggregate large email lists with avid genre readers and email those readers daily or weekly with book recommendations. These services build a reputation on providing solid book recommendations to their subscribers, so if they recommend a book, their subscribers will likely buy it.

I hope you can see why this is such a lucrative business model for marketers and an effective marketing strategy for authors.

For a fee, you pay the email promotion service to list your book, and you agree to price your book at $0.99 (or another discount price). In return, the email promotion service will promote your book on the day of your promotion.

The most common technique that authors use is "ad stacking," which means chaining different email promotion newsletters together during a short period to maximize your book sales.

Here is an example of how ad stacking works:

- On Sunday, Service A lists your book.
- On Monday, Service B lists your book.
- On Tuesday, Service C lists your book.

And so on. My recommendation is to book your promotions one day and one service at a time so that you receive sustained exposure for your book over your promotion period. Usually, most promotions last at least a week, so you'll want to stack your promotions at five to seven services.

Also, it is not always easy or possible to do this, but I also recommend stacking the smallest services earlier in your promotion and the biggest services at the end of your promotion. This is because Amazon favors books that sell with momentum; if Amazon sees your book sales growing in a straight line, it is going to pay more attention than if your sales are growing in spikes.

Other retailers don't use algorithms like Amazon's and tend to reward you much more if your book takes off. But because a large percentage of your sales is likely to come from Amazon, and many email promotion subscribers are Amazon shoppers, you can't afford to avoid paying attention to the Amazon algorithms when ad stacking.

Ad stacking has made me a lot of money over the years, and I'm confident it will do the same for you too.

PAID ADVERTISING

You can also purchase pay-per-click advertising. Most authors use Amazon, Facebook, BookBub, TikTok, and Pinterest ads at the time of this writing, but it seems that there are always new services offering ways to reach their readers through paid methods.

With pay-per-click advertising, you create an ad that the platform serves to thousands, if not millions, of readers. You only pay when someone clicks on your ad. The hope is that enough people click and buy to make your ad spend profitable.

Pay-per-click advertising is one part science and one part art, and it is not for the faint of heart. If you've never used it before, you are almost guaranteed to lose money unless you invest in a paid course to help you understand the fundamentals of this unique marketing method.

I like pay-per-click advertising, but I didn't understand it when I started. I thought I could experiment my way to success, but I failed miserably. It was only when I purchased a $300 course that taught me the ins and outs that things finally clicked for me. I wished I had purchased the course much sooner.

Take my advice: pick one platform, invest in a premium course to learn pay-per-click advertising on that platform from someone with a track record of success, and pay close attention. It will save you a tremendous amount of money.

Once you learn how to use pay-per-click advertising platforms, you'll find that they are more similar than different. I learned through Amazon ads. That made my transition to Facebook ads much easier, for example. Pick one platform and master it before adding another.

Some tricks that have helped me master pay-per-click advertising include:

- improving my copywriting skills
- improving the quality of my marketing graphics through purchasing stock media rather than trying to create something myself
- keeping my bids low, then scaling them accordingly
- watching my budget like a hawk
- being willing to lose money in exchange for data (the more clicks you receive, the more data you have about why something is working and not)
- organizing my dashboard into portfolios that help me understand how groups of my books are performing
- keeping a journal of what I tweak and when
- tweaking only one item at a time, even if it takes a while to determine if and when something works

My final tip is to be patient. It took me several months to achieve profitability on my first pay-per-click advertising platform; now, I am profitable on all pay-per-click advertising platforms. I am proud of that because I know most authors lose money in this endeavor. Just know that profitability is possible for you too, but you will have to sacrifice some time and money to get there.

SPEAKING

Public speaking is a fantastic way to improve your book sales if you have the right personality and the right books.

Public speaking can come in many formats:

- podcast interviews
- author readings
- in-person or virtual speaking events

In any case, speaking is not for everyone, but I have used it to great effect throughout my career. In fact, I have become so adept at speaking that I am always in-demand. I have only ever pitched to speak at an event once, for 20Books Vegas, which the organizer accepted. All of my other speaking leads have come through organic word-of-mouth.

First, it goes without saying, but you must have a book that is worth speaking about and/or a dynamic personality. Nothing is worse than listening to an author drone on and on about their books, especially when they take forever to get to the point. If you can master public speaking, you will have an advantage because most authors steer well away from it. After all, public speaking is one of the most common fears among humans!

Here are my top tips to develop a career as a speaker and land engagements that will help you sell more books.

A SPEAKER'S PAGE

In the website chapter, I discussed the importance of developing a press page highlighting your accomplishments in case someone wants to feature or interview you. If you want to be a speaker, I recommend modifying your press page with a few extra items to attract speaking engagements.

First, let the world know you are open to speaking at events. That is an obvious tip, but it's amazing how frequently it gets overlooked.

Next, implement a time service on your page for speaking engagements. For example, I inform event organizers that I will respond to their invitations within 24 hours. When I receive an invitation, I stop what I'm doing to review it. I take pride in giving organizers fast answers. If the answer is yes, they will know within a day. If the answer is no, they will also know within a day so they can move on to the next person. This is professional courtesy, and if you give them a fast no, they will remember that and be more likely to invite you to another event, assuming you are a good fit for each other.

Next, I also recommend including a demo reel on your speaker's page. A demo reel contains clips from events you have spoken at that will show organizers what you would be like as a speaker at their event. I recommend keeping your demo reel to around two to three minutes, and I recommend that you use your best content only. An alternative is to post a video of a speaking engagement you did in the past (but only if the organizer permits it). This is another great alternative.

I have a YouTube channel, which is a great source of leads for me. I frequently receive invitations to speak at events because organizers stumble upon my YouTube videos. That has worked amazingly well for me. You don't have to start a YouTube channel, but you should consider how organizers will come across you in the wild. They need great content, so you need to show them that you are a world-class professional at giving them good content.

Last, make sure your contact form is always operational. Contact forms break all the time, and you don't want to be in the unfortunate position of receiving an invite to a dream event, only never to see it!

WORKING WITH EVENT ORGANIZERS

In this chapter, when I refer to "an organizer," I mean anyone asking you to speak at their event or platform. This includes podcast hosts and physical or virtual event organizers too.

My best advice for working with an organizer is to be the easiest person they have ever worked with. You would be surprised how many personalities organizers have to deal with. They have to put up with speakers who don't reply to their emails in a timely fashion, jerks, prima donnas, and other disorganized people. If you can avoid being all those people, your organizer will remember you fondly. They'll remember you as someone they enjoyed working with, and you will probably be invited back or promoted to another organizer. Organizers can and do talk.

Here's how you can be the easiest person to work with:

- Reply to emails quickly.
- Keep your emails professional and succinct.

- If you must negotiate something, be professional about it.
- On the day of the event, be punctual.
- Read every email the organizer sends you at least three times, and make sure that you do everything they tell you to do.
- If anything the organizer says is unclear, ask them about it early.
- Anticipate what the organizer will need, and then have it ready when they ask (i.e., headshots and author biographies).
- Give a great talk.
- Follow up and thank the organizer after the engagement.
- Be kind and gracious at all times.

It's not complicated. But you'd be surprised how many people struggle with these things. Make sure you don't struggle with them, and you will find organizers ready and willing to work with you.

SOCIAL MEDIA

Next up is a hot topic in every writing circle: social media. Either you've got it figured out or you're trying to figure it out.

I'm not a social media master. Far from it. My social media skills aren't the best in the world, but somehow I've amassed around 40,000 YouTube subscribers at the time of this writing, so I must be doing a few things right.

DEVELOP A SOCIAL MEDIA STRATEGY

First, don't talk about your books constantly, please. I beg you. It doesn't matter what social media network you choose; authors will always be spamming their books. In fact, I'll create a new law right now.

Michael La Ronn's Law of Social Media: if you search for writing on any social media network, within two minutes, you will see an author spamming their work.

No one likes the "buy my book" schtick. It looks cheap, and readers will hate you for it. I'm not saying *not* to promote your work on social media...but every five minutes is a bit much.

I follow Gary Vaynerchuk, an entrepreneur, internet

marketer, and investor. I like Gary a lot despite his sometimes profane language and brutal honesty. He said early on in his career that you should use social media to document your journey. Don't worry about monetizing or squeezing money from your audience. Document your journey to becoming whatever you want to become. Open the door and show people what it's really like. That's precisely what Gary has done, and it's why he's a multimillionaire with his social media ventures at the forefront of his businesses.

If you have followed me for a little while, then it should be no surprise that my personal social media strategy is to document my journey.

My YouTube channel documents the lessons of a working writer.

My podcast, The Writer's Journey, documented my day-to-day life from 2018 to 2021.

My book series for authors, *Indie Author Confidential*, chronicles the lessons I've learned as an indie author.

In short, I'm following Gary Vaynerchuk's advice, though it's not on the "true" social media networks like Facebook, Twitter, and so on.

If you choose to use the traditional social media networks, what's your plan? It doesn't have to be anything like mine. It could just be to share whatever's on your mind at any given time. But it helps to have a plan, because you really shouldn't promote your book with every post. And yes, I'm using the prescriptive *should*. Few things in life are absolute. Spamming your books on people is absolutely not a good idea.

IF YOU DON'T HAVE ANYTHING NICE TO SAY, DON'T SAY NOTHIN'

As my grandmother used to say, hold your tongue. Avoid negativity, especially against other authors. It's not worth it. Keep your brand on social media positive, respectful, and professional, even when it's tempting to deviate from it.

Avoid commenting on other authors' activities that you don't agree with. It will only hurt you in the long run.

Once, I knew someone who suffered severe bullying on Facebook. Back when "writing on people's wall" was the fashionable thing to do, and before Facebook implemented the news feed, the way you browsed Facebook was to pick people's profiles and see what was on their wall. This person had a lot of hateful stuff on their wall. They told me they chose to leave the hateful comments on the wall as a testament to the haters' bad behavior, that maybe someday it would come back to haunt them. To me, the comments were nothing better than graffiti.

Making negative comments about other people on *your* social media network is like spray painting your front porch with ugly, vomit-colored spray paint. It will be there for your readers to see...forever.

PICK THE PLATFORM THAT SPEAKS TO YOUR PERSONALITY

Which social media network jibes best with your personality?

For me, it's YouTube and Twitter. For others, it might be Instagram. Your personality is probably different from mine. Experiment with the platforms to find the one you enjoy most, which also nets you the most engagement. Then double down, learn the inner workings of how to be successful on the platform, and try to duplicate the behaviors of successful influencers there.

KEEP TALKING, EVEN IF NO ONE LISTENS

Many people start on social media but give up because no one sees their content. It makes you feel like you're creating content and sending it into a black hole.

But keep talking, even if no one listens. Even if you gain a few followers a week, that's okay. If you're consistent and create good posts, at some point, your following will grow. Keep experimenting with different ways to reach people and engage them.

When I started my YouTube channel, I had zero subscribers. If I was lucky, I gained a subscriber a week during the first few months. I kept creating, even when it felt like no one was listening, and now I have over 40,000 people who tune in to watch me every week. I wanted to give up when I had 100 subscribers. Thank goodness I didn't.

Building an audience takes time. Be patient, keep creating, and keep talking, even if (you think) no one is listening.

HAVE FUN

This is probably the most recurring tip in the book, but that's because I believe in it. If you can't have fun doing something, it's not worth doing. That includes social media.

If you struggle to create content that you or your audience enjoy, you're probably not having fun anymore. Your audience can tell. Stay authentic, stay true to yourself, and beware of trolls.

SOCIAL MEDIA WELLNESS

We need to talk about social media wellness. Ironically, it's still somewhat of a fringe topic. At the time of this writing, people will still look at you funny if you put social media and wellness in the same sentence, but in the future, people will realize how dangerous these networks can be to our mental health. Social media has a dark side and can ruin people's lives. And no, I'm not trying to bash social media networks because it's fashionable. They do a lot of good, but the companies are not responsible for the power they wield in our lives.

The point of this chapter is not to scare you, but to make you aware. For example, on a Friday night, have you ever opened up your favorite social media network with the intent of checking it for just a few minutes, only to find yourself still there an hour later? That's by design. Social media apps are engineered to keep you on the platform as long as possible so that they can gain data about your browsing habits to sell to advertisers, so advertisers can show you ads that create more data about you...

As the trendy saying goes, when a product is free, *you're* the product.

On the one hand, this is a force for tremendous evil, particularly during political elections. On the other hand, it's how honest people make their entire living. I myself benefit tremendously from social media advertising and YouTube ads. So...I'm conflicted. You probably are too. That's why staying balanced is critical.

LIMIT YOUR TIME ON SOCIAL MEDIA NETWORKS

When you open an app to check it for a few minutes, *check it for a few minutes and get the hell off.* It's hard, but do it. Otherwise, you'll lose entire days to social media. I know I have.

Before I realized what was happening, I can't tell you how many times I'd get lost in a rabbit hole on YouTube. I'd start off watching writing videos, and then somehow end up on weird politics channels. This is because YouTube knows me better than I know myself when it comes to my tastes (sometimes). It serves me content that it thinks I will like. I wasn't aware of this for *years,* and I let YouTube take me on weird rides. Now I'm aware of it. I recognize that the YouTube algorithm serves me great content, but it can also serve me content that is not good for me. Therefore, I choose when I want to let the algorithm serve me, not the other way around.

Limit your time on your networks and engage with them on your own terms.

Another personal tip: avoid social media as much as possible around major political elections. Regardless of what your political feelings are, 2016 taught us that bad actors are trying to manipulate *everyone* regardless of your political affiliation. It'll be better for your mental health if you can avoid social media altogether during the month before the election.

AVOID COMPARISONITIS

Social media sites are like casinos. They keep you coming back. Instead of spending money, you spend attention. And the house always wins. There are many interviews with ex-social media engineers who admit that the websites are engineered to maximize your time on the platform. It's also similar to how processed foods are engineered to make you want more with each bite. You can't eat just one potato chip, for example.

There are increasing numbers of studies linking social media to anxiety, depression, and paranoia. The 2019 pandemic didn't help the situation.

And we haven't even gotten to the main topic of the tip yet, which is comparisonitis. If you have warts, you don't want social media to see them. You're going to photograph yourself in the best possible light. Same with social media. No one shows their warts. They'll show you pictures that make it look like they have a perfect life, even though it might be in shambles. That beach photo of your high school acquaintance might have been taken just before they had a nervous breakdown, but you'd never know it. They look so happy!

I'm not trying to be overly negative, but social media brings out an interesting aspect of human nature: if people have to choose what to show the world, they're going to show it the best possible situations. Few people will go on social media to talk about their struggles. Some will, but it's not the norm. Therefore, you will always have a warped perspective of what someone's life is like. There are no exceptions to this, myself included, though I try to be balanced.

When everyone around you is living seemingly perfect lives, and yours isn't perfect, it's awfully easy to compare yourself to them and think about how deficient you are. It creates the urge to "keep up with Joneses" and chase status symbols. It's a vicious cycle where everyone loses, and it's one of the major drivers behind the increasing anxiety, paranoia, and depression that social media is causing.

BE CAREFUL WITH YOUR DATA

Remember that your data is a commodity and can and will be weaponized against you by *someone*. Be it the opposite political party to which you are affiliated or a marketer trying to prey on your dreams and fears, it will happen at some point. In the legal world, when the police arrest someone, they say, "Anything you say can and will be used against you in a court of law." In social media, assume that your data can and will be used against you in the form of advertising.

If you understand this, then you'll know when you're being manipulated. My goal is for authors to understand how to use social media on their own terms. That Kickstarter ad on Facebook that you're seeing? Maybe it's perfect for you. But tap on the ad intentionally rather than doing it without understanding how the greater forces behind the scenes are at work.

As a marketer, this is also paradoxical. As a user, you want to protect your data, but as a marketer, the data social media companies provide are extremely lucrative. We wouldn't be able to run Facebook ads without it, for example. I view this as one of the most interesting contradictions of modern marketing. You should at least be aware of it when you're marketing.

BE POSITIVE

Social media amplifies negativity. Negative posts tend to do better because they receive more engagement and mobilize crowds.

This isn't unusual for social media networks. Isn't it also true that bad news gets more press than good news? The news media will plaster a serial killer's face all over the five o'clock news; a child cancer survivor who starts her own lemonade stand? Nope, unless there's no better news they can find.

Social media network algorithms are engineered to promote the posts with the most engagement, not necessarily the negative ones. But because the negative posts receive the most engagement *because of human nature*, they're overrepresented and typically what you see more of. This leads to the impression that you must be negative on social media to get attention. Positive posts are less popular.

However, your main goal should be to be positive, even if it's not algorithm-friendly. Build your brand on positivity, not bashing others or reverting to the mean, even if it is financially more lucrative. Perhaps this makes me a contrarian, but I care about building a long-term career, and I imagine you do too.

BE WARY OF GROUPS

Social media communities are a great place to connect with other people, but these groups are also where the ugliest traits of humanity live. Block anyone and everyone who doesn't treat others with respect, and leave toxic groups.

A typical social media writing group usually has the following timeline:

•A few people start the group and derive mutual benefit from communicating with each other, usually by trading marketing advice.

•More people join, and the group grows quickly. This is the golden age of the group. Everyone is positive, the good advice flows, and everyone is happy. Members check the group several times daily because they don't want to miss anything.

•Then, trolls join. Or some of the original members become trolls. All it takes is one or two people to poison the place. Factions form over minor disputes.

•*Something* happens that creates differing opinions among the group. The trolls mobilize their factions, and suddenly, everyone is at each other's throats. Many of the original members who joined during the golden age leave in outrage. All that's left is a toxic atmosphere where you'll find an occasional tip. But mostly, you'll find pure beginners who have no idea what the place used to be like and are asking questions that the group was never intended for, and you have trolls who antagonize any and everyone who doesn't agree with their agenda.

•The group dies.

I haven't seen a writing community that doesn't succumb to this life cycle. This is why I no longer participate in writing groups. They appeal to human character flaws that I prefer to not be around. My time is better spent writing.

If you engage in communities, do it on your own terms, and

don't waste your time in communities when more important things are calling, like writing and marketing.

If you *start* a community as part of your platform, be especially wary of this life cycle and do what you can to head it off, especially if you become very successful.

A GREAT BOOK ON SOCIAL MEDIA WELLNESS

I highly recommend *Ten Arguments for Deleting Your Social Media Accounts Right Now* by Jaron Lanier. Lanier is a philosopher and computer scientist who has been sounding the alarms on the dangers of social media for years. It's essential reading if you want to understand how social media networks are engineered to keep you hooked, and what you can do about it. I don't recommend deleting your accounts as Lanier does, but I do recommend being vigilant.

SHORT FICTION

Short fiction is a wonderful way to market and promote your work to readers if you do it correctly.

Many magazines publish short stories by authors. Submit your stories to these magazines for consideration. These magazines, like email newsletter promotions, have built a reputation on providing quality fiction to their subscribers. If a reader picks up the magazine, reads your story, and likes it, then they will want to explore more of your work.

Another great thing about short fiction is that it doesn't require as much commitment as a novel. Readers read stories faster, and if they like one of your stories, they will probably like your novels.

Even better, many magazines pay authors for their stories, so magazines can also be a revenue stream!

However, the most difficult part about short stories is writing them. I began my career with short stories but found it difficult to get back into the short story mindset when I transitioned to novels. Now, I write them regularly, but it was an adjustment. Fortunately, it wasn't a difficult adjustment, but it required time, energy, and focus.

This chapter will quickly cover the craft, business, and marketing of short stories.

WRITING SHORT STORIES

Authors squabble about what the length of a proper novel should be all the time, but the universally-accepted length of short stories is well settled. According to the Science Fiction Writers Association (SFWA), a short story is anything less than 7,500 words. Anything under 1,000 words is generally considered flash fiction, and anything over 7,500 words is usually novelette or novella territory. Try if you might, but those are facts. A short story is anything between 1,000 and 7,500 words, though the sweet spot is usually somewhere between 3,500 and 5,000 words.

You should aim for the sweet spot.

If you want to submit your work to magazines, my experience is that most magazines don't accept anything over 5,000 words. A few outliers will accept up to 7,500, but with a story that long, you are limiting the markets that will consider your work.

You can never go wrong with a story that is 4,000 to 5,000 words long, but, as they say, your story should be as long as the story needs to be. Don't let length dictate your content, but do try to control this where you can.

One way to do this is to use the Lester Dent Plot Formula. This was created by Lester Dent, who was a prolific and very successful pulp writer. Dent used this formula for his novels and short stories, and his formula is popular among professional writers.

In the Dent Formula, you divide your story into four parts. Dent worked with a 6,000-word story as the basis for his example, but I use 5,000.

Each part is 1,500 words. Dent provides the beats of exactly what needs to happen in each section. In short, you start with your hero in trouble, and you ratchet up the trouble and make it worse as the story progresses.

When I first started writing, I didn't know about the Dent Formula, so my stories were very short—around 2,000 words max. That's not enough time to develop a character or build a world. The story really doesn't have heft until it surpasses 3,000 words in my opinion. Once I switched to the Dent Formula, my stories got longer, and editors started to pay more attention. It was like magic. In fact, one of the first short stories I wrote under this method was immediately purchased by an editor! If that's not a good testimony, I don't know what is.

Whether or not you follow the Dent Formula, you still need a well-written story that falls within the length sweet spot of what editors are looking for.

Other craft tips for writing short stories include:

- The scope of short stories doesn't need to be as big as that of novels. Often, the hero solves one problem and does not save the world.
- Short stories are great ways to practice your fiction. Use them to practice writing in a new genre, a new craft technique, or a new type of character.
- Use section breaks to your advantage.
- Read published short stories by professional authors in your genre to understand what short stories feel like. I like to group them into two categories: highbrow and lowbrow. Highbrow fiction (regardless of genre) has a more serious feel. The level of writing is top-notch, and the writers usually cover deep topics. Lowbrow fiction is fiction that doesn't take itself too seriously. That's not to say that

it's funny, but it is lighter and more focused on entertaining the reader than making them feel a particular emotion. My earliest stories were exclusively lowbrow, but I have found that paying magazines want highbrow fiction. Now I write a mixture of both. You'll have to make that decision for yourself.

- Make sure your story can be slotted into a clear top-level genre (science fiction, fantasy, mystery, horror, and so on). It will make it much easier to market that story to editors.
- If you write speculative novels, then, as much as possible, make sure that your stories are also speculative.
- Short stories that take place in your character's world are also a smart idea, but don't go overboard.
- When formatting your short story, use the Shunn Manuscript Format. No exceptions, unless a specific magazine wants something different.
- Have fun writing short stories.

THE BUSINESS OF WRITING SHORT STORIES

So, you want to license your stories to magazines. Great!

We will assume that you have at least one story that you're ready to submit.

First, let's discuss what you are licensing to magazines. Rather, what you *should* be licensing to magazines.

People often say that they "sell" short stories to magazines, but that's not really what happens. When an editor agrees to buy your work, you don't give them the copyright, so the verb "sell" is inaccurate. Instead, you license *your story to an editor for a short time.*

Magazines typically take first serial rights, which means they are the first venue to publish a story. When you license first serial rights, you agree that your story will appear exclusively in that magazine for the first time. After publication, the rights revert back to the author. Some editors ask for an exclusivity period, such as three months or six months before reverting the rights back to the author. But the point is that the rights revert back to the author. You do not give them away.

You license first serial rights in exchange for a fee, which is usually a payment by the word. At the time of this writing, the SFWA states that a "professional" magazine must pay at least $0.10 per word. Any market that pays less than that is considered "semi-professional." Any market that pays significantly less than that is considered "token."

So, if you sell a story to professional magazine, you will make at least $0.10 per word. Pretty cool!

Which magazines should you submit your work to?

Personally, I only submit to professional markets. I would much rather be paid for my short stories, and if a magazine doesn't want a story, I would much rather self-publish it and give it to my audience.

Some people enjoy submitting work to semipro and token markets, and that's fine. Make the best decision for you, but remember that you can and should be paid for your work, especially if it gets published in a large magazine.

The good thing is that professional magazines are reputable and ethical, and you don't have to worry about your business dealings with them. Many publish templates of their standard author contracts online for you to review. If you don't like it, then just don't submit to that magazine.

Now that we've gotten business stuff out of the way, let's talk about the submission process. To find magazines, use a website like Ralan.com or Duotrope to find magazines that publish work in the genre of your story. Both of these websites break down magazines by genre, payment level, and the type of content they publish, so you can find good candidates quickly.

Develop a short list of magazines that could be a fit for your work. Review their websites, read sample copies of the magazine, and read their submission guidelines very carefully. If you determine that a magazine is a good fit, you must follow its submission guidelines.

If a magazine says that it only wants science fiction, then only send science fiction. If the magazine doesn't want stories over 5,000 words, then don't send them a 6,000-word story. In other words, follow instructions and don't be an idiot. If you read editorial guidelines, you can tell editors deal with their fair share of idiots. Once you make a bad impression, that's it. You will probably never be considered for that magazine again. Don't do silly things to help you stand out other than follow the instructions and write a really good story that the editor will want to buy. It's that simple and that hard.

If you plan on submitting multiple short stories to the various markets at the same time, then I recommend developing a system to stay organized. Most magazines do not allow simultaneous submissions, meaning you will have to submit your stories to one magazine at a time, wait for acceptance or rejection, then submit them to the next magazine. When you consider that magazines take several weeks or months to reply, then you need to be extremely organized so that you do not send multiple submissions to a magazine, or worse, accidentally perform a simultaneous submission.

There are two ways to do this.

The first is to track your submissions manually, either by hand or using a tool like Microsoft Excel. The second way is to use a submission manager like Duotrope. You still have to track your submissions manually in the submission manager, but it provides a clean way to do so without having to worry about building a tool yourself.

I personally use and recommend Microsoft Excel because I am comfortable with Excel, but I know that Excel and writers don't always mix. Look into both methods and figure out what works best for you. The key is to develop a system that keeps you organized.

As you write a new short story, put it on your tracker and wait for the rejections and acceptances to roll in!

MARKETING SHORT STORIES

Let's say you send as many stories as possible to different magazines, and you receive an acceptance! Congratulations! That's fantastic news. Let's discuss optimizing the situation so you do not miss any opportunities.

First, negotiate your rights properly. Make sure you lock down your contractual obligations, copyright terms, and payment. If you get published by a professional magazine, all of this is usually a formality.

Second, consider what type of short story it is. Does the short story jibe with your main genre as an author? For example, if you specialize in space opera, does your story take place in space and match the general tone of your longer works? There's no wrong answer here, but your strategy will differ depending on your response to the question.

If the answer is yes (the story matches your dominant genre), then that's great news. If readers love your short story, then they will probably love your long-form works too. I would strongly recommend including the name of any related series titles in your author bio. I also recommend mentioning your genre in the author bio. This way, readers will have a specific thing to look for, reducing missed opportunities.

If the answer is no (the story does not match your dominant genre), then that's not bad, but you should still point future readers to any works that would be a good jumping-off point from the story. For example, let's say that you're a genre hopper. Your dominant genre is science fiction, but a magazine accepts your fantasy story. If you have any fantasy series published, send magazine readers to those. They may not be interested in your science fiction. This is obvious, but you would be surprised how frequently this does *not* happen. Often, what happens is that readers will find a story they love, but then not know where to go next. With a little forethought, you can eliminate this problem.

If you sell other short story collections, consider routing magazine readers to those instead of your novels, assuming there is a genre match. You never know what kind of mood the reader will be in—they might only want to read short stories when they encounter you. Give them options.

If you publish a story after publication (whether individually or part of a collection), make sure that you let readers know where it first appeared. This is usually done on the copyright page. You should also include copy in your book description, like "Published in X Magazine!" to add more hype to your sales copy.

Follow these tips and you will be in a great position when you receive an acceptance.

Remember, stay inside readers' heads and keep in tune with what they might feel when they read the magazine. It will help you sell more books.

Nothing is worse than a reader reading one of your stories in a magazine, loving it, but not having a clear idea of how to engage with you next. Make sure that doesn't happen.

MISCELLANEOUS MARKETING ITEMS

In this chapter, I will cover some miscellaneous marketing tips that didn't fit elsewhere in the book. Hopefully, these will be good food for thought.

AUTHOR COLLABORATIONS

I'll start this chapter by saying that anything is possible with author collaborations. Everything I list in this chapter is just a suggestion, not the end all, be all. In fact, sometimes the best collaborations are the most creative ones, so read this chapter and start mulling over some ideas.

In an author collaboration, both authors pool their talents and resources to promote each other's works.

Here are some examples of author collaborations I have seen and done in my career so far.

COWRITING

Writing a book together is a fantastic collaboration idea, though it is not without pitfalls. In a cowriting arrangement, two or more authors write a book, sell it to their audiences, and split the royalties. In theory, this is simple, but in practice, it is anything but. For example, who writes which chapter? Who handles the editing? Who handles the cover design? What happens if one author doesn't fulfill their obligations under the contract? What happens if the authors have a disagreement? What happens when one author dies?

As you can see, numerous issues must be addressed with a solid contract. Otherwise, this method isn't worth it. Remember that you and your coauthor will own the copyright to the book that you co-create for your lives, plus 70 years. That is a long time to be in business with someone, especially if you disagree with them. This is why I only recommend cowriting in situations where you know the other author very well. You must both be on the same page about everything, and you must both have the same level of professionalism. Otherwise, you are setting yourself up for long-term trouble.

NEWSLETTER SWAPS

As I've discussed a few times in this book, it is always a good idea when authors cross-promote each other's books to their mailing lists. It requires minimal time and effort and doesn't cost anything. Make sure that the author you collaborate with also writes in your genre and subgenre. Otherwise, the promotion won't be nearly as effective.

BUNDLE-LIKE PROMOTIONS

With this method, one author serves as a host. This author creates a page on their website featuring the books of other fellow authors. During a mutually agreed time, all the authors agree to discount their book to $0.99 and notify their mailing lists accordingly. This functions very much like a bundle, except readers can choose which books they buy and where.

MUTUAL LINKS

If you develop a really good relationship with a fellow author whose books are similar to yours, consider including a permanent link on each of your websites to the other's work. This will grant exposure over time.

BLOG TOURS

Many authors have blogs and often feature fellow authors' works. This is another great way to cross-promote, especially if you organize a "tour" where you appear on multiple blogs during a promotion period.

BOX SETS AND BUNDLES

A box set is a collection of books by a single author or multiple authors in which the books are provided at a discount.

In the case of a box set by an individual author (read: you), you include a collection of novels, preferably the first few books in a series or the entire series itself. You then price the book so that it is more attractive for readers to purchase than the individual volumes, usually with a discount of at least ten percent.

I don't recommend selling box sets on Amazon at this time because, as discussed in the pricing chapter, you earn only a 35 percent royalty when you price your book over $9.99. Instead, I recommend selling box sets everywhere except Amazon so you can take advantage of the higher royalties that other retailers provide over $9.99.

In the case of a box set by multiple authors, this is a collaboration in which each author provides a short story or novel. The box set is usually priced at $0.99 as a promotion, and each author featured in the box set promotes it to their audience during the promotion.

Box sets are an excellent way to cross-promote. They're not as effective as they used to be, but they are still effective, especially if many authors are featured in the set.

The bundle is a collection of novels by multiple authors where readers purchase the bundle, but the books are provided separately. Honestly, the only difference is that a box set contains all of the novels in one file; with a bundle, you usually receive each book separately, but in the same folder.

Many authors have used box sets to grow their careers. Others have used them to hit bestseller lists like the *New York Times* and *USA Today*.

There is nothing inherently wrong with this marketing method, but do recognize that it can be used for evil. For example, some authors charge an extraordinary amount of money to participate in a box set with the promise that the box set will hit a bestseller list. Be careful about paying money to be in a box set. I don't recommend it.

When used properly, box sets are killer marketing tools.

BUSINESS CARDS

Business cards are vital. Most authors treat them like an afterthought. How will people remember your name and face if you attend an author conference? Think about the last event you attended; could *you* to recall every person's name and face? Of course not, so why wouldn't you bring business cards?

Now that we've settled that business cards are required, consider taking an additional step. Include your face on your business card. Think about it. You'll meet so many people throughout an event that you will not remember their faces. But if someone puts their face on a business card... You get the idea.

Also, don't forget to put your phone number on your business card. I've talked to many authors who think this isn't necessary anymore, but unless you want to miss opportunities, you should include it. You never know if or when opportunities will come in the form of phone calls. Once, I received a phone call out of the blue that I answered with suspicion. The person on the other end introduced themselves as an event organizer. They had met me at a prior conference and wanted to know if I would be interested in speaking at theirs. I said yes in a heartbeat. That encounter taught me the value of including your phone number on your business cards. If you don't want to share your real number, sign up for a free Google Voice account. Problem solved.

(A word of caution: answering phone calls is always a good idea, but if Hollywood comes knocking, conduct the conversation in writing. In some cases, due to California law, you could accidentally give away your copyrights over the phone!)

EMAIL SIGNATURES

Your email signature is also prime real estate that you may be neglecting.

Think about how many emails you send every day for your author business. Why not put a link to your website and the cover of your newest book in the email signature? Hire a designer on a site like Fiverr to do this for you cheaply. It's painfully easy.

This is a low-cost, easy marketing tactic that you can do today. Then, when you email someone, they'll see your face and a link to your site. They just might click to see what you have to offer.

SHORT NONFICTION

Just as short fiction can be a great marketing tool, so can short nonfiction.

If you write nonfiction, consider writing short works that promote work at the end. Ideally, this short work should be tied to your nonfiction work.

For example, I have written guest blog articles for various websites and magazines in the writing niche. These short articles have helped me grow an audience because they provide value. Even if your niche isn't writing, there are probably places you can pitch to write short articles, assuming they allow that sort of thing.

You'll find that there is a burgeoning market for short nonfiction too. It will ultimately depend on your niche and how popular it is.

Don't rule out short nonfiction, because it can be lucrative, and it can help you grow your audience. The short fiction chapter's recommendations about working with an editor, rights licensing, and article submissions also apply to short nonfiction.

CROWDFUNDING YOUR BOOK

Many authors are now using crowdfunding services like Kickstarter to fund the production of their books. This is a great idea to build buzz, fund your book, and service your fans.

Many courses and resources can help you run a successful crowdfunding campaign. Just do a simple web search. I have not yet had the opportunity to do a crowdfunding campaign myself, but my work has been part of a few Kickstarter campaigns.

Here are my tips for getting started with a successful crowdfunding campaign:

- Write and finish the book before you ever think about running a campaign. If your book isn't finished, don't waste readers' time.
- Spend the money upfront to produce your book's e-book and paperback versions. Don't ask readers to do this. If your crowdfunding campaign successfully funds, great—if not, you still need to publish the book anyway.
- Messaging is everything. Approaching a campaign from the perspective of "I have a new series that I

would like to share with you" is much better than "Help me fund this series so I can publish it." Don't offload responsibilities to your readers. You'll come off as looking desperate.

- Be creative with your stretch goals.
- Study other successful crowdfunding campaigns to determine best practices.
- Listen to interviews and take courses from other authors with a track record of successfully funding their campaigns.
- Invest the time to create nice graphics and a short video to promote the campaign.
- Write captivating sales copy!

That's a good start. There's no doubt in my mind that any author can use crowdfunding to build an audience and defray some of the costs of publishing. Any money you can save is a great thing, but you also want to make sure that you give your audience appropriate rewards and fulfill those rewards on time.

PUTTING IT ALL TOGETHER: THE ULTIMATE BOOK LAUNCH

Everyone wants to know how to do stellar book launches. It's one of the top marketing questions I receive.

I'd like to offer several inconvenient truths:

1. Unless you have a killer book and the right personality, a massive book launch will likely waste time and money until you have more books and a larger readership.
2. A variation on the first truth: the bigger your audience is, the easier it is to do book launches.
3. The idea of a book launch comes from traditional publishing, where publishers pool all of their resources into a book's launch to give it the best possible chance of success.
4. In traditional publishing, if a book doesn't do well at launch, the publisher doesn't attribute any more money to it. The book is no different from a spoiled banana.

5. As a self-published author, your books don't spoil. You will earn money on them for your entire life and 70 years after your death.

For the sake of argument, let's say that you publish a book at age 25, and you die at age 75. That's 50 years. Add another 70 years to that, and you have 120 years, which is 43,800 days. Yet, here some authors are, worried about the first 30 days of their book launch and calling their book a failure if it doesn't become a bestseller during that period. The first 30 days are just the first 30 days.

I know people don't like to hear these truths, but they are important. Don't stress out over your book launches. Often, there's not much you can do about them early in your career.

Here is a simple book launch strategy when you have more books to your name and a bigger readership. Think of it as the ultimate low-cost, low-effort book marketing and promotion checklist.

Prep Work

- Determine the genre and subgenre of your book.
- Determine comparable books.
- Use everything you know to create an effective cover.
- Write excellent sales copy, and don't leave it to the last minute.
- Use tools like Publisher Rocket to research your book's best categories and keywords (and Amazon Ad keywords too).

- Make sure bookstores can purchase your book through Ingram and that you have the correct discount enabled.
- Optimize your back matter with a strong call to action.
- Determine a launch date in advance. How far in advance you want to go is up to you, but let's say 90 days.
- Reverse engineer every marketing and promotion tactic you want to do, determine how long it will take you to prepare, then mark your calendar accordingly.
- Stick to your calendar.
- Use preorders if you want, but make sure you understand the pros and cons.

Your Website

- Create a dedicated book page on your site for your book, with clean URLs for as many retailers as possible.
- Geo-locate links wherever you can so readers will be taken to their country's version of their preferred retailer.
- If your book is available in a special format like audio or large print, put that on the book page.
- Embed a sample on your website using a tool like Amazon's embed tool so readers can start reading directly on the page.
- If you have an audiobook, embed an audio sample on your book page.

- Feature the book above the fold on the home page of your site.
- If you run a promotion where the book is priced lower than full price, then consider putting a visible timer on the page to instill a sense of urgency for readers. Let them know when the sale ends, and let the clock compel them to buy.
- Feature your newest book in the sidebar of your blog.
- If you have a blog, share your book on your blog.
- Find other non-obtrusive ways to feature your book on your site.

Your Newsletter

- Optimize your mailing list opt-in on your site to prepare for new prospects visiting your site.
- Create a compelling lead magnet that will entice readers to sign up for your list (if you haven't already).
- Notify your mailing list subscribers about your book.
- Consider creating an autoresponder promoting the book.
- Orchestrate newsletter swaps with other authors.

General Promotion

- Create nice marketing graphics for your book.

- Use every tool retailers give you.
- Set up an ad-stacking campaign.
- Run paid advertising to the book and adjust your budget accordingly, depending on your results.
- Order a handful of paperback copies and donate them to your library, Little Free Libraries, and coffee shops and hotels with complimentary bookshelves.
- Ask your existing fans for reviews.
- Use review services such as Book Sirens and Book Sprout to gather as many reviews as you can as early as possible.
- Consider trade reviews if you plan to aggressively target bookstores and libraries.
- Share your book several times on social media, but don't be spammy about it.
- Distribute your book as far and wide as you can in as many formats as you can manage so that readers worldwide can buy your book at any time.
- Line up as many cross-promotions with other authors in your genre as you can, including but not limited to newsletter swaps, box sets, and bundles.
- Take advantage of each retailer's marketing tools to help you improve your sales around the world.
- Consider finding blogs and/or podcasts willing to talk to you about your book.
- If appropriate, consider a trade review.
- Write a short story in the book's universe and submit it to professional magazines to see if any will accept it.
- Update your email signature and possibly your business card with your book's cover.
- Finally, write the next book.

. . .

Writing that next book is important because it begins the cycle anew.

Remember, focus on things within your control. Everything I listed in this chapter is 100 percent within your control. You don't have to do them all.

Book launches can be intimidating and stressful. Try to have some fun. After all, you only launch a book once!

If you need more clarity on the terms I've used in this book, turn the page to read a glossary that I put together for you.

I hope this book taught you something and gave you some marketing tactics that you can get excited about. Good luck out there, and I wish you all the best.

Remember, this is a long-term game. I hope to see you at the end of the road.

GLOSSARY

ADVANCED READER COPY (ARC)

1. A pre-publication copy of an author's book sent to readers to secure early reviews, feedback, and buzz

AFFILIATE MARKETING

1.Revenue-sharing arrangement where individuals ("affiliates") are paid commissions for selling and promoting the products and services of other businesses

The most popular and internationally-recognized affiliate program in the world is Amazon Associates. Nearly anyone can sign up to be an Amazon Associate, and they can include Amazon affiliate links on their website—if someone clicks on an affiliate link and buys anything on Amazon, the associate receives a small commission because the theory is that they helped create a sale where one wouldn't have existed otherwise.

While Amazon is the most easily understood example of affiliate marketing, many entrepreneurs pay affiliate commissions for their products, services, and online courses, usually offering affiliates free copies in exchange for a review. The affiliate then makes commissions on any future sales they refer.

Affiliate marketing can sometimes involve ethical and legal perils. Some countries like the United States legally require affiliates to disclose any affiliate links and/or whether they received a product for free to avoid misleading customers.

While affiliate income may not be as lucrative for books, writers can still make affiliate income by promoting books, products, and services that they use or enjoy to their audiences.

AUTORESPONDER

1. Sequence of automated emails sent to mailing list subscribers that educate them on a topic

2. An automatic email that lets email senders know that you are unable to respond to email (known as a "vacation responder" or "out-of-office reply"); popular in email clients

For definition #1, an autoresponder is also known as a follow-up. Autoresponders are an effective email marketing technique. Their power lies in their automation and the ability to set rules. Many authors time autoresponders to send every few days for a set period to help new mailing list subscribers learn more about the author and the books they write. They can even create conditional autoresponders that go to a subscriber if they take a certain action, like clicking on a specific link in an email. When written authentically, they help keep readers "warm" until an author has a new book to share.

For definition #2, just know that some people may use the

word autoresponder to refer to an out-of-office email, particularly in the corporate world.

BLURB

1.A short testimonial by an author or a reader that praises a book

2.Another term for a book description (incorrect)

While the term "blurb" is often substituted for a "book description" in everyday conversation, that usage is not technically correct. Merriam-Webster defines "blurb" as "a short publicity notice (as on a book jacket)."

A blurb can appear on the front or back cover of a book, in the front or back matter, on a book's product page, or in any other place where the author is trying to promote their book.

Also known as an endorsement quote.

BOOK INDUSTRY STANDARDS AND COMMUNICATIONS (BISAC)

1.A universal metadata classification system used by bookstores and online retailers to organize books

BISAC codes were developed by the Book Industry Study Group (BISG), a trade organization to help standardize the transfer of book metadata across the industry. They ensure that bookstores and publishers speak the same language when classifying books for sale.

Any given BISAC code consists of two parts: an alphanumeric code and a genre descriptor.

For example, as explained on the BISG website, a travel book that takes place in the southern United States would have the alphanumeric code TRV025070 and the genre descriptor TRAVEL / United States / South / General. The most important part of any code is the descriptor, because the descriptors are the categories that writers select when they upload their books to book retailers. Almost all retailers use the BISAC codes to organize their books for readers to browse. Some, like Amazon, use the BISAC codes as a starting point and have additional categories that authors can use.

BOX SET

1. A compilation of several novels, novellas, or short stories by different authors, usually created for the purpose of cross-promoting similar authors to a target audience; may be short-term or long-term

Indie authors didn't create the box set, but they certainly reinvented it. The technique is most commonly used by indie authors to create exposure for their books. Unlike an anthology, a box set does not usually have an editor, but there may be a foreword by a famous author, and the existence of more popular authors is almost always used to draw readers to help them discover lesser-known authors in the collection.

BUNDLING

1. The act of selling different books or items together as a package

BUYER PERSONA

1.A fictional representation of an author's target reader, their demographics, buying behaviors, and preferences based on real data

Also known as a customer avatar or reader persona.

Buyer personas are frequently used by businesses to get into the heads of their customers so they can market to them better. By creating an ideal customer profile, they can design products with the buyer persona in mind.

CALL TO ACTION (CTA)

1. A compelling argument to get a customer to do something that will solve a problem they have, such as buying a product

CAMPAIGN

1.A one-time newsletter sent to an online mailing list
2.A limited time in which an ad is served to an audience ("ad campaign")

Definition #1 (a one-time newsletter) is also known as a broadcast or newsletter. The terminology depends on the email provider.

. . .

Also known as a sales handle.

CATEGORY

1.Division in an online retailer where a book is located

Usually, category is synonymous with genre, but they are not always the same. For example, a poetry book written by Maya Angelou would be located in the poetry category at whatever online retailer you buy it. But the book would also be placed into subcategories based on what is available under the BISAC system. In Maya Angelou's case, poetry can be categorized by the ethnicity, gender, or the author's nationality, so the category listing for an e-book written by her might look like this: Poetry / American / African-American or Poetry / Women.

On almost all online retailers, bestseller lists are organized by categories.

CLICK RATE

1.An email marketing statistic that measures the percentage of people who click a link in any given newsletter or autoresponder

2.In advertising, the percentage of people who click an ad, most commonly known as a click-through rate

The click rate is important because it measures how well your email copy entices your readers to take action. You want your readers to open AND click on the links in your emails.

A high click rate indicates that readers are reading your emails to the end and clicking through to wherever you want them to go (such as the product page of a new book). A low click rate indicates weak copy. You may need to adjust your messaging, sentence length, paragraph pacing, and even your call to action to improve it.

CONVERSION

1.In formatting and publishing, the act of transforming an e-book from one format into another (such as ePUB to MOBI)

2.In marketing, the transformation of a prospective customer into a buying customer

See *Call to Action, Click Rate, Impressions, Pop-Up, Sales Funnel, Split Test,* and *Mailing List.*

CONTENT MARKETING

1.A style of marketing where marketers promote products via content such as blogs, podcasts, and online videos, and where the product itself is not the sole focus of the content, but an important element

COPY

1.In advertising, the written words in an advertisement
2.In publishing, the text of a book

In a digital age where consumers are bombarded with ads, more brands have turned to content marketing because the content is a softer pitch, is shareable, and can often stand on its own.

In 2017, the US fast food chain KFC released a romance

novel called *Tender Wings of Desire* with its iconic Colonel Sanders as the lead. KFC released the book in honor of Mother's Day, a historically high sales day for the franchise. The book went viral, and according to many, the book was actually pretty decent. This is content marketing at its finest.

A more common example of content marketing is a lawn care blogger talking about their weekly lawn care, and how they use a certain organic fertilizer because of how the fertilizer aligns with their strategy of not using too many chemicals on the lawn. The fertilizer discussion is just one part of the overall theme of the video.

CROSS-SELL

1.The act of an author selling other products to a reader either before, at, or after the point of sale

A classic example of cross-selling is an "Other Books by the Author" page in the back matter of a book.

Cross-selling can also involve products other than books. For example, if the author sells t-shirts or other merchandise and promotes those to readers, that's also cross-selling.

CROWDFUNDING

1.The act of raising money from an audience to fund a project
2.The act of patronage from fans (such as through Patreon)

Crowdfunding has grown in popularity in recent years as creators use the power of their audience. For example, if an author wanted to fund the creation of a graphic novel edition of their book, they may ask that their audience make donations to a Kickstarter campaign to help pay for it. In exchange for donating, the author may give readers bonuses such as free copies of the work, access to behind-the-scenes footage, and unused art.

FIRST RIGHTS

1.The exclusive right to publish a work for the first time

Literary magazines commonly purchase first rights for short stories so that they are the first ones to print the work. Traditional publishers also buy first rights to the novels they publish (among many other rights).

HOUSE AD

1. An ad that you run on your own website to promote one of your books or services

IMPRESSIONS

1.The number of times an ad is served (but not necessarily seen)

INDEPENDENT BOOKSTORE

1.An independently-owned bookstore that is self-reliant in bringing customers into the store

Your local bookstore is an independent bookstore. Your local Barnes & Noble/Chapters/Waterstones/etc. is not. They are franchised and can draw upon the power of their brand and ability to open very large locations at malls and shopping centers to bring in foot traffic. A local independent bookstore doesn't have that kind of capital or power, but it does have knowledgeable booksellers who can provide better service and choices for readers.

INFLUENCER

1.An individual with a large following on a blog, podcast, or social media site, usually with the ability to influence their followers to buy or not buy a product, and to act or not act upon something, such as a petition

INTERNATIONAL STANDARD BOOK NUMBER (ISBN)

1. A unique numeric identifier attached to a book that makes it possible to be found in databases

INTERNATIONAL STANDARD BOOK NUMBER (ISBN)

An ISBN has several uses. For starters, you need one to have your book distributed into physical bookstores.

However, for e-books, they are optional, as all retailers will let you publish without one.

If you do use an ISBN, you are required to use a different ISBN for each edition of the book, meaning if your book is available in paperback and audio, you would need to use a separate ISBN for each.

ISBNs can have 10 or 13 digits. Much like a VIN on a car, each digit has a meaning, but that's outside the scope of this book.

ISBNs are country-specific and can only be issued by an appointed agency in each country.

Nielsen provides reports on the publishing industry each year, and they base their reports on books that have ISBNs, including e-books. As a result, since many indie authors do not use ISBNs for their e-books, the indie world is somewhat of a "shadow industry" that isn't tracked on any official reports.

Unlike the Amazon Standard Identification Number (ASIN), an ISBN can be used on any retailer. The only caveat is that some retailers such as Amazon and Draft2Digital issue free ISBNs if the author doesn't have their own, which makes it easy to publish on those retailers—but the catch is that the retailer will be listed as the publisher of record for the ISBN, not the author. As such, for competition reasons, other retailers won't accept an ISBN with another retailer's name on it.

KINDLE DIRECT PUBLISHING (KDP) SELECT

1. Amazon's exclusive publishing program that offers algorithmic and marketing benefits (including Kindle Unlimited) for a book in exchange for exclusivity to the Amazon ecosystem

LAUNCH

1. The process of making a book public for the first time

Launches are important events in the life of every book. Authors usually plan them weeks if not months in advance so that they can book promotions at promo sites, arrange newsletter swaps, send advance reader copies to early readers and book bloggers, and other promotional activities.

A "hard launch" is when the author communicates the

book's release immediately when it becomes available. A "soft launch" is when the author publishes the book, but waits a period to start talking about it while they wait for early reviews and sales. The goal of a soft launch is to have some social proof before the major promotions begin.

LAW OF DIMINISHING RETURNS

1. In any given business activity, when the amount of return is more than the money invested, but with repetition becomes less profitable

A classic example of diminishing returns with indie authors is with book promotion sites. You can only promote your book to the same group of people before they tire of it. The first time you promote a book to a list of readers, you may see a nice sales bump. But the next time you promote that book, you'll usually see fewer sales.

LEAD MAGNET

1.In marketing, a free item that a business gives away to entice customers to sign up for an email list, such as a white paper, free book, or webinar

In the writing community, lead magnets are referred to as "reader magnets," popularized by Nick Stephenson's book *Reader Magnets*.

For authors, a reader magnet is usually a free book or a short story.

LICENSE

1. The right to use a copyrighted work for a certain purpose; granted by the copyright holder

In legal terms, licensing is also known as encumbering.

LIFE-OF-COPYRIGHT CONTRACT

1. A contract that is valid for the entire life of the copyright of the work

Life-of-copyright contracts can be devastating for a writer. It is best to avoid them at all costs.

LIST HYGIENE

1. The act of purging your email list of subscribers who no longer engage with emails

LIST PRICE

1. The recommended retail price (RRP) of a book, set by the author or publisher

LOSS LEADER

1.A product sold at a loss to attract customers

Grocery stores use loss leaders all the time, such as buy-one-get-one-free offers on certain foods to get shoppers in the store. Once shoppers are in the store, they'll usually spend more money, which will help the grocery store make up for the loss leader.

Authors do this primarily through steeply discounting an introductory book to a very low price or free.

MAILING LIST

1.An email list where subscribers sign up for updates from a business, usually in exchange for a free gift

Also known as a newsletter or fan club.

MERCHANDISING

1.In book sales, the act of hand-selecting books to be featured prominently in a bookstore or an online retailer
2.In business, the act of creating affiliated products such as t-shirts, cups, mugs, or other products associated with a business's brand beyond their flagship products or content

For definition #1, merchandising is how bookstores make their money. By featuring some books at the front of the store, they could sell more of them. The same goes at online retailers—any time you see big banners advertising new series or "summer reads," that's merchandising.

For definition #2, merchandising and creating different types of products is a great way to create another income stream.

METADATA

1.A set of data that describes other data

When you upload your book to sell through a retailer, you must enter certain items: title, author name, book description, keywords, etc. Each of those elements is metadata. It describes your book so that 1) the retailer can place it in the appropriate place on a physical or digital shelf, and 2) so readers can find your book, know who wrote it, and what it is about. Don't ignore or underestimate the power of metadata, especially your book description, keywords, and categories. They can help your book be discovered.

MODEL RELEASE

1.In photography, a waiver of liability granted by a model in a photo shoot so that the photographer has the right to use their photo for commercial purposes

Model releases are important for authors in a couple of areas. First, it's always best practice for a cover designer to use stock photo images for which a model release exists. Some retailers even keep releases for photographers.

If the model is a minor and the photographer didn't realize it, or the model claims that they did not authorize the sale of a stock photo and selling it is an invasion of their privacy, this protects the author, the cover designer, and the retailer where the designer purchases the image.

Second, a model release is important when an author is buying stock photo images to use on their blogs, ads, etc. Knowing that a model in a given stock photo has released their rights is an added layer of assurance that the retailer has the right to license the image, has secured the appropriate permissions, and that there is no risk of copyright infringement. While model releases are not always possible to get, they are important.

OPEN RATE

1. An email marketing statistic that measures the percentage of people who open any given newsletter or autoresponder

OPT-IN

1.The act of granting consent to a business to send communications, usually emails

Opt-ins are a must in today's digital economy where people are protective of their email inboxes. Businesses offer a number of incentives to customers in exchange for their email, such as coupons, free content, and free services. Email lists are valuable because the business can email its customers any time it has a new product or major announcement, thus improving sales.

A "single" opt-in is when a customer must enter their email address once in order to receive the incentive. This usually happens on the business's website, and once done, the customer is on the email list.

A "double" opt-in is when a customer must enter their email address and then click a link via email to verify that the business does in fact have their permission to email them. Double opt-ins are more work for the customer, but the business can be certain that their customer list has given them permission to communicate.

Failing to obtain customer's permission before emailing is illegal in some countries and can even lead to lawsuits. Legal consequences or not, it is generally frowned upon and unethical.

See *Mailing List* and *Opt-Out*.

OPT-OUT

1.The act of unsubscribing from a business's email list

Also known as unsubscribe.

Customers may choose to be on a business's email list for any reason, and they may also choose to leave for any reason. Businesses usually offer a way for customers to "unsubscribe" and stop receiving emails. Many businesses track their unsubscribe rates as an indicator of whether their email content is relevant.

As with opt-ins, failing to offer an easy way to unsubscribe can also result in broken laws and lawsuits.

ORGANIC SEARCH

1.The act of users entering a search term in a search engine and happening upon content naturally

Also known as natural search. Organic search is important because it's free. You don't have to pay for it. If you have a tea review blog, customers are searching for "tea review blogs," and they happen to find your blog and consume your content and become a fan, your customer acquisition cost is zero. You didn't need to pay for an ad to drive traffic to your website.

For fiction writers, the only organic search they'll likely enjoy is when readers are searching for their name or one of their books.

For nonfiction writers, organic search should be a key pillar in the discoverability strategy. Nonfiction writers can create blog articles, podcasts, and videos that speak to topics that people their target market are actively searching for.

PASSIVE INCOME

1.Income derived from activities that do not require ongoing effort

Passive income activities usually involve creating content once and letting it work for you, such as releasing a video that promotes an affiliate link. In fact, affiliate income is one of the most lucrative passive income strategies because you can create a lot of content around certain products, and automate the traffic to them through ads.

As a personal aside, I make affiliate sales from videos I made YEARS ago.

Other examples of passive income include low-maintenance online courses, and of course, book sales, though one could argue that book sales are passive-aggressive—if you don't do something to market your books, they will eventually fall off the radar, but even if you do nothing, you'll still probably sell some.

PAY-PER-CLICK ADVERTISING

1. Advertising structure in which businesses bid for keyword search terms to appear high in search engine results; businesses pay every time a prospective customer clicks on the promoted link to their website or product

PERMAFREE

1. A book that is permanently free (a permafree book)

Authors may choose to make a book permafree as a loss leader to get the book into readers' hands in exchange for sales down the road. This is typically (and most effectively) done with Book 1 in a series.

PLATFORM

1. An audience of interested people around a cause
2. A social media website or tool an influencer uses to reach an audience

PRESS KIT

1. Kit that contains relevant marketing information about a business

Also known as a media kit. Businesses commonly host a press kit on their site that includes product specs, press releases, photos of a product in different dimensions, and other interesting items that journalists can use to write feature articles about the product.

Authors can use press kits to feature themselves and their books to make it easy for a blogger or podcaster to cover their book.

PRICE ANCHORING

1. The act of using an initial price to influence a buyer's perceptions on the value of a product

Here's a great example of price anchoring: "I normally charge clients $99 for this course. But because I want you to be successful, and because it's Black Friday, I'm offering it for just $67."

By establishing the $99 price, everything that comes after will automatically sound cheaper.

Price anchoring is often a common tactic on sites with tiered plans; the most popular plan will be highlighted to draw your eye to it. Once you see that first, you'll automatically judge all the prices on the page.

PRICE-MATCHING

1.The act of one retailer matching another retailer's price for a given book, usually by algorithm

Amazon uses a price-matching to ensure that it has the best prices. For books, if it detects a lower price on another retailer such as Kobo, it will automatically drop the price of the book on Amazon to match the price.

SALES FUNNEL

1.Series of steps that lead a customer from a less expensive (or free) product to a more expensive one

A proper sales funnel might look like this: an entrepreneur has a free podcast with great content that entices listeners to join their email list. When listeners join the email list, the entrepreneur sends an autoresponder sequence that promotes a cheap product (say $10). If the customer buys that product, after a certain amount of time, they receive another autoresponder sequence that promotes a more expensive course, say $500. From the very beginning, the sales funnel is designed to lead them toward the course.

SEARCH ENGINE OPTIMIZATION (SEO)

1.The process of using search engine best practices to improve a website's chance of ranking high in organic searches

SEGMENTATION

1.In email marketing, the act of separating email subscribers into groups based on their engagement, demographics, actions they've taken in the past (such as buying a product), or some other metric that is important to a business

Let's say that you have an email list of 1,000 subscribers, but you have a problem: no one seems to be opening your emails. So, you segment the subscribers who haven't opened your email into a separate group so that you can email them one last time to try to reengage them.

Let's say that you have an email list with 10,000 subscribers, and you want to advertise your newest product only to those who bought your last book. You can segment those people into a separate list.

Segmentation is effective because you can view open and click rates for that group in isolation compared to your overall list, which may be helpful in many situations.

How segmentation works ultimately depends on the email service provider, but most providers allow you to do it some shape or form. It has many practical uses.

SOCIAL PROOF

1.External validation of a creator's content through public fan support, such as product reviews, number of followers, social media shares, etc. (both in quantity and quality)

SQUEEZE PAGE

1.On a website, a landing page intended solely to convince visitors to take an action, such as joining a mailing list

A good squeeze page has the following elements:

•A great headline that catches the viewer's attention
   •Convincing sales copy
   •No navigation or any other links. The viewer must take the action you want or leave the website.
   •Pleasant images or video
   •A call to action. Depending on what the action is, it may be repeated throughout the page. Most authors won't do this unless they are selling an informational product.

SPLIT TEST

1.The process of testing one or more versions of content to see which performs better

Also known as A/B testing.

Split testing is commonly done with email marketing, web advertising, copywriting, and anything that is customer-facing. The goal is to optimize an ad, image, or piece of content to its fullest potential so that it converts at the highest rate.
   Common things authors can split test are book covers, book descriptions, and ads through Facebook or Amazon.

Split testing can be done manually or through specialized apps and services.

STOCK CONTENT

1. Photos, graphics, audio, and video that can be purchased royalty-free for use in a creator's content

UPSELL

1. The act of promoting upgrades or add-ons to a customer at the point of sale to increase profits

"Would you like to Super-Size your fries and drink?"

That's a line formerly used at McDonald's to upgrade customers from regular-sized fries and sodas to gigantic ones that defined fast food restaurant portion sizes for decades. It's a classic upsell, perhaps one of the most famous of all time.

"Would you like to add the extended warranty for your computer for an additional twenty dollars?"

You get the picture.

Upselling differs from cross-selling in that the goal is to improve or complement the products that the customer is already buying. With cross-selling, you're selling them another product entirely.

MEET M.L. RONN

Science fiction and fantasy on the wild side!

M.L. Ronn (Michael La Ronn) is the author of many science fiction and fantasy novels including *The Good Necromancer*, *Android X*, and *The Last Dragon Lord* series.

In 2012, a life-threatening illness made him realize that storytelling was his #1 passion. He's devoted his life to writing ever since, making up whatever story makes him fall out of his chair laughing the hardest. Every day.

Learn more about Michael
www.authorlevelup.com (for writers)
www.michaellaronn.com (fiction)